A TRIBUTE TO
DALE
EARNHARDT®

David Taylor/Allsport

Commemorative Edition

A Tribute To Dale Earnhardt®

Photo Credits
Front cover (left to right): Jamie Squire/Allsport, David Taylor/Allsport, AP/WWP
Back cover: John Cordes/ICON SMI

EDITORIAL		ART	
Managing Editor:	Jeff Mahony	Creative Director:	Joe T. Nguyen
Associate Editors:	Melissa A. Bennett	Assistant Art Director:	Lance Doyle
	Gia C. Manalio	Senior Graphic Designers:	Marla B. Gladstone
	Mike Micciulla		Susannah C. Judd
	Paula Stuckart		David S. Maloney
Assistant Editors:	Heather N. Carreiro		Carole Mattia-Slater
	Jennifer Renk		David Ten Eyck
	Joan C. Wheal	Graphic Designers:	Jennifer J. Bennett
Editorial Assistants:	Timothy R. Affleck		Sean-Ryan Dudley
	Beth Hackett		Kimberly Eastman
	Christina M. Sette		Melani Gonzalez
	Steven Shinkaruk		Jim MacLeod
			Jeremy Maendel
PRODUCTION			Chery-Ann Poudrier
Production Manager:	Scott Sierakowski		

R&D

Product Development
Manager: Paul Rasid

ISBN 1-58598-165-6

306 Industrial Park Road
Middletown, CT 06457
www.CheckerBee.com

Table Of Contents

A Tribute To
Dale Earnhardt®

Three. When this edition of the CheckerBee Fan Guide™ series was planned, it wasn't supposed to be like this. No, at the age of 49, Dale Earnhardt was still at the top of his game, with no sign of the end of his reign of intimidation. This guide was to be a celebration of Earnhardt's remarkable – and ongoing – career. This was to be an exploration of the phenomenal success and popularity of an incredible NASCAR driver.

CY CYR/NEWSPORT

This was to be for the fans – to enhance their enjoyment of a man who commanded the respect of the racing world.

Three. That's where Earnhardt should've placed in the 2001 Daytona 500. It wasn't in Earnhardt's nature to be satisfied with third place, but this time was different. He had welcomed Michael Waltrip onto his team, a driver who had never won a Winston Cup race in more than 400 starts, and his turnaround would be so swift and complete that he would win the BIG ONE in his very first race with the Earnhardt team. Earnhardt's son, Dale Jr., would finish second in the race and make his daddy proud. And Dale himself would personally escort them to glory, and Earnhardt and his team would finish 1-2-3.

Three. That's the number of words we had to add to the title of this book when tragedy struck. A Tribute To . . . It wasn't supposed to be.

But, you know what? When we lifted our heavy hearts and built this tribute to good old #3 – it was still the glorious book it was meant to be. It *is* a celebration of Earnhardt's remarkable career – a career that will forever reverberate in our hearts and memories. It *is* an exploration of the phenomenal success and popularity of an incredible NASCAR driver. It *is* for the millions and millions of fans – to celebrate the amazing accomplishments of a man, a hero, a legend.

We will miss you Dale. You will not be forgotten.

The Man In Black

Dale Earnhardt® – An American Legend

Dale Earnhardt truly was an American legend. With seven racing titles under his belt (a feat that only he and Richard Petty have accomplished), Earnhardt was undoubtedly the best driver of his day. A shrewd businessman who was among the first to capitalize on his name and image, Earnhardt made millions and became one of the most recognized men in the business. Even for those who didn't know the difference between a lug nut and a walnut, the mention of "Dale Earnhardt" was enough to conjure up the image of this tough competitor with the cowboy mustache, the mirrored sunglasses and the smirking grin.

The Legend

But while his image was one of the most recognizable in the nation, Earnhardt's private nature made him one of the hardest drivers to know off the track.

Isaac Hernández/Mercury Press

The intimidating black Monte Carlo was an unwelcome sight to any competitor.

In fact, Dale Earnhardt was an incredibly complex man. To the world of racing, he was the Man In Black, a mysterious figure whose fans were some of the most loyal in the crowd. To his competitors, he was the road bully known as the Intimidator who wouldn't hesitate to edge an opponent off the track to win a race and yet served as a generous mentor to countless drivers who looked to him for advice. He was the "good old boy" from the rural South who lived his entire life in the same region, yet helped to make NASCAR a national phenomenon. He was a multimillionaire who owned a jet, fishing yachts and acres of land, yet he still rose at the crack of dawn to do hard labor on his Mooresville, North Carolina, farm.

Whether race fans loved him or hated him (and there were plenty of both), no one could deny that Dale Earnhardt was the man who made racing fun. He never regretted smashing a competitor out of the way, and never complained when someone else did that to him. In fact, he even

If you can't stand the heat, stay out of the kitchen: Tony Stewart takes to the air as hard-driving Dale Earnhardt races past.

coined his own term, "Earnhardting," which referred to a driver who ruthlessly bumped a competitor off the road.

For Earnhardt, a casual race totally defeated the point. He raced to win. But he also raced because he loved every minute of it.

> "If people think Dale is tough, they should have raced against his daddy."
>
> — Ned Jarrett, who was a racing rival and a friend of Ralph Earnhardt during the late 1950s

Every time The Intimidator seemed to be all washed up, he'd speed back into Victory Lane again. Despite his vastly successful career, Earnhardt won the Daytona 500 only once in his 25-year career. During his years on the NASCAR circuit, he enjoyed more cheers and endured more jeers on the track than just about any other driver in history. But that was OK by the fans. They just wanted to see The Man In Black race, whether he won or not. After all, the Earnhardt family has had racing in its blood for generations.

Like Father, Like Son

Just like his father Ralph, Earnhardt enjoyed a successful career racing stock cars.

During a 1998 interview, Earnhardt was asked how his family felt about his eminently hazardous job. His characteristically deadpan response was, "Well, they started it. I mean, Dad raced, so why can't I?"

It's true that Dale's father raced, but his mother, Martha, certainly was not pleased with her husband's chosen career. When Ralph Earnhardt first told his young wife that he wanted to race stock cars, Martha tried to talk him out of it. "When Ralph started [racing], I was only 19 years old and I really didn't have sense enough to worry," she told the *Charlotte Observer* in 1998. "I thought, 'Well, he's lost his mind.' [Although] I threatened to leave, he just kept talking. So I decided if I couldn't beat him, I guess I would have to join him. I didn't want to leave him, really." They may not have known it at the time, but Ralph and Martha Earnhardt's agreement on racing was the beginning of three noble generations of racing legends.

On The Road Again

Dale Earnhardt's hometown of Kannapolis, North Carolina, honored its favorite son in 1993, when it renamed a stretch of highway (where, incidentally, the famous driver used to get speeding tickets) Dale Earnhardt Boulevard. "I used to go bird hunting with my father at the end of that road," said The Intimidator at the dedication ceremony.

For years, Ralph Earnhardt tore up dirt tracks all over the Carolinas and Georgia with his signature #8 car, hogging roads and trading paint with the likes of Ned Jarrett and the young Richard Petty. Like most drivers in the 1950s, he wouldn't hesitate to knock you off the road if you happened to get in his way. (Years later, many of these seasoned drivers would see their old rival Ralph in Dale Earnhardt's style of track showdowns.) Ralph's prowess would win two NASCAR Sportsman Division titles, back in the days before the Winston Cup became the ultimate prize.

Earnhardt's father also possessed amazing mechanical skills. In the garage behind the Earnhardt home, he crafted some of the finest stock car innovations of the 1950s, being the first driver to use roll bars and tire stagger. He even made a name for himself building and modifying race cars for other drivers, earning him the eternal gratitude of the sport he helped create.

"My dad was the biggest influence on me," The Intimidator would later say. "He taught me that if you want to do something bad enough, you can. And you can be good at it if you work hard."

Hometown Boy

Already blessed with two daughters, Ralph and Martha's first son came into the world in Kannapolis, North Carolina, on April 29, 1951. Named Ralph Dale Earnhardt, the boy was exposed to the automotive world immediately. As a boy, Earnhardt spent most of his time in his father's garage, and had little interest in being anywhere else.

Later on, the Earnhardt father and son would race against each other only once, on a local dirt track. "[M]y dad, who was leading the race, came up behind me [after lapping the rest of the field] and I couldn't figure out what he was doing," Earnhardt said in 1996. "Finally, he started bumping me, so I figured I better hold the car straight. He pushed me by this guy and I beat him, then dad drove on past me." Even though he wanted to help his son in the race, Ralph Earnhardt still made sure he took first place himself. His son came in third.

Racing cars had become as much of a passion for Dale as it had for his father, and that passion far outweighed his interest in school. To his parents' distress, young Dale would eventually drop out of ninth grade to race beat-up jalopies on the local dirt tracks. He would later deeply regret leaving school, but never his reasons for it.

He may have owned a hauler with his face plastered on it, but Earnhardt remained a hometown boy.

AP/WWP

Dale Earnhardt® – An American Legend

FAN CHECKERBEE GUIDE

Building a dream out of engine blocks and lug nuts wasn't an easy task for a teenager. Earnhardt took his father's knowledge and tried to make that dream a reality while working through a series of dead-end jobs. Installing insulation at a local textile mill may have helped Earnhardt pay the bills, but he certainly knew he didn't want to make a career out of it! Ralph Earnhardt had always taken care to put his family's needs before his racing, but his son was determined make a

Earnhardt's son Kerry (left) also has tested his mettle in the world of stock car racing.

living behind the wheel. The man who would later earn a reported $40 million throughout his career often had to borrow money from the bank on Friday, desperately hoping the weekend's race would win him enough money to pay back the loan on Monday. And with a wife and a son, Kerry, by the age of 18, Earnhardt's debts only got deeper.

But his trademark determination finally got Earnhardt the chance to rebuild a car owned by one of his neighbors in 1969. The 1956 Ford Victoria wasn't much to look at, but Earnhardt and his crew diligently worked on it before finally finishing it. They didn't have enough money for a proper paint job, and The Man In Black made his track debut in a car painted pink! But the color hardly mattered when he took fifth place at Charlotte Motor Speedway in Concord, North Carolina. It seemed the "cottonhead from Kannapolis" was ready for NASCAR.

Tragedies

Personal setbacks postponed Earnhardt's racing debut, however. His first marriage broke up, and it would be several years before he and Kerry would

be close again. A marriage to Brenda Jackson failed too, after producing a daughter, Kelley, in 1972 and a son, Dale Jr., in 1974.

The most tragic event of Earnhardt's life came in 1973. After driving his way into legendary status and teaching his son the stock car racing ropes, Ralph Earnhardt died of a sudden heart attack. Years later, Dale Earnhardt would own the Chevrolet pickup that he and his father were rebuilding at the time – the last thing father and son had done together. "He was my hero," Earnhardt once told an interviewer about his father. "To this day, I still use the things he taught me. In my opinion, he was the greatest. What I have, I owe in large part to him. And what I have, I would give up to have him back."

Earnhardt's racing success coincided with personal tragedies.

Robert Laberge/Allsport

The Big Break

After driving in the Sportsman Series with his father's honored #8, Earnhardt finally got a crack at NASCAR in 1975. Car owner Ed Negre was willing to let him drive a Dodge Charger at the 1975 World 600 at Charlotte Motor Speedway. Sadly, he finished in an embarrassing 22nd place. Then again, it's hard to finish well when you're racing against the legendary Richard Petty!

But it would still be three years before Earnhardt would finally break into the Winston Cup series full time – three uneventful years of driving second-rate vehicles for various team owners, and getting nearly nothing out of it. But Rod Osterlund, who owned a formidable racing team of his own, noticed Earnhardt's impressive attempts in 1978. When Dave Marcis quit the team late in the 1978 season, Osterlund knew just who could replace him. After nearly a decade of driving jalopies and rebuilt cars around dirt tracks and playing second fiddle to accomplished NASCAR drivers, Earnhardt was finally able to drive a higher class of cars for a real team.

> **A Word From Our Sponsor**
>
> Earnhardt's sponsors before driving for Rod Osterlund included the U.S. Army, Hy-Gain and the Cardinal Tractor Company.

Lucky In Love

Earnhardt's personal life also began to take a turn for the better. With two divorces behind him before he was 30 years old, Earnhardt probably did not think that he could find someone special. But that all changed when he met Teresa Houston.

Teresa, like her future husband, was accustomed to the world of auto racing – she came from a family of racers, too. Her father, Hal Houston, had raced the short tracks along with his brother Tommy, so a man who lived for the track was nothing new to her. Earnhardt and Teresa hit it off and the match between the two of them would develop into one of the most successful partnerships in NASCAR history – both in business and in love.

Earnhardt proudly holds his trophy for the International Race of Champions on August 4, 2000.

AP/WWP

Off To A Great Start

When he finally got the chance to hit it big in NASCAR, 27-year-old Earnhardt gave an impressive showing in his first season. While driving a Monte Carlo for Osterlund, he got his first win at the Bristol Motor Speedway in Tennessee, after zooming ahead of Darrell Waltrip and Bobby Allison to take

Earnhardt's wife Teresa played a big role in his success both on and off the track.

the checkered flag at the 1979 Southeastern 500. A ruptured tire at Pocono led to a broken collarbone and temporarily put him out of commission after that year's Coca-Cola 500, but the young newcomer impressed everyone when he returned to race at Richmond. He ended the season with 11 finishes in the top five and 17 finishes in the top-ten, an amazing debut that led to a Rookie of the Year title for Earnhardt. Not a bad start for a first season!

If a Rookie of the Year award was an achievement, the next year would be even better. Even though pit crew chief Jake Elder quit mid-season, Earnhardt's impressive five wins and great finishes put to rest the rumors that the Osterlund Racing team was a flash in the pan. Most importantly, they led to Earnhardt's first Winston Cup championship, the first of the seven, which would make him a NASCAR legend. No one in the history of NASCAR had ever earned Rookie of the Year and the Winston Cup title in consecutive seasons! The victories led to Earnhardt's first major sponsor, when Wrangler Jeans approached the team. At the time, the future looked bright.

Minor Setbacks And
Major Accomplishments

But then Rod Osterlund replaced the winning Chevys from the 1980 season with Pontiacs and by mid-1981, Osterlund sold the team to J.D. "Jim" Stacy. Within a month of the sale, an unhappy Dale Earnhardt quit the team to join the brand-new racing team owned by recently retired driver Richard Childress.

After an unsuccessful career that included no wins at all, Richard Childress had decided to leave the driver's seat and try his luck with owning a team instead. But Earnhardt's time with Childress didn't last long either, because the new team lacked the funds and equipment to propel

Read all about it! Dale Earnhardt is the 1980 NASCAR champion.

Earnhardt to victory. Childress encouraged Earnhardt to work with a more experienced team and, in 1982, Earnhardt and his sponsor, Wrangler, were driving for Bud Moore's shop. For the next two years, Earnhardt would be driving Ford Thunderbirds and achieving few victories. The only bright spot of the 1982 season turned out to be his victory at the Rebel 500 at Darlington.

But even if his racing career wasn't the best at the time, fate was about to hand Earnhardt something he needed far more than victories. While recuperating from injuries sustained from crashing into Tim Richmond at the Mountain Dew 500 at Pocono, Earnhardt finally proposed to Teresa – from a hospital bed, no less. When she accepted, it would be the start of a whole new life for Earnhardt. He was also able to gain custody of Kelley and Dale Jr. in 1981, something he had struggled to do for years.

The partnership of Richard Childress (above) and Earnhardt proved fruitful for both men.

Back To Basics

Earnhardt left Bud Moore after the 1983 season to go back to Richard Childress. He brought the Wrangler sponsorship with him, opening up the possibility for better cars with more money. However, Wrangler also had a contract with Bud Moore's team, so race fans saw two Wrangler cars hug the curves in 1984 as Ricky Rudd took over Earnhardt's #15 Ford, and Earnhardt drove a car with the number that would make him famous. It was the #3.

Although 1984 was, as he and Childress called it, "a rebuilding year," Earnhardt was able to pull himself out of his previous slump with wins at Talladega and Atlanta. A year later, new crew chief Kirk Shelmerdine helped the team improve their short-track performances. During that season, Earnhardt earned his reputation as a rough driver by trading paint multiple times with Tim Richmond. "I think he'd have tried to do the same thing," Earnhardt said after sending Richmond out of control during a race at Bristol. "Anyone would. If they say they wouldn't, they're lying."

> "I fell in love with Teresa when I found out she fixed her Pinto after it overheated . . . that's an independent woman!"
>
> — Earnhardt on his wife Teresa

Richmond didn't seem bitter either. "I'm not mad," he told the press after Earnhardt bumped him out of the lead. "It was good, hard racing, and I knew what to expect."

Friends And Enemies

Although it would take The Intimidator two decades of racing to finally win the Daytona 500, it certainly wasn't for lack of trying. His lead in the 1986 race ended when, of all possible things to have happen, he ran out of gas! Despite that loss, Earnhardt would take home his second Winston Cup in 1986, and a record-breaking season earnings of $1.7 million! He certainly needed that money, since that was the same year he

Crew chief Kirk Shelmerdine was instrumental in the rebuilding efforts of Richard Childress.

was fined $5,000 for clipping Darrell Waltrip at Richmond. The rivalry between Earnhardt and Waltrip would go down in NASCAR history as one of the fiercest ever seen. But, ultimately, the rivalry proved to be only on the track, as Darrell would go on to cheer for his younger brother, Michael, who became a driver for Earnhardt's team in the year 2000.

Family Ties

While Earnhardt was burning rubber and trading paint in the 1980s, he and his family began to reconnect with his oldest son. Kerry Earnhardt had been living with his mother and stepfather and, although he knew perfectly well who his biological father was, the two never had much to do with each other. In fact, Dale Jr. never even met his half-brother until he was in his early teens. But Earnhardt eventually began spending more time with Kerry, and the Earnhardt boys – Kerry and Dale Jr. – bonded as well, both launching racing careers of their own. Kelley would also dabble in racing, and there are some who say she could have raced rings around both of her brothers if she had pursued it!

When Teresa became pregnant in 1988, Earnhardt knew that he had the chance to be the kind of father he hadn't been able to be for Kerry, Kelley and Dale Jr. With a renewed enthusiasm for his family, Earnhardt threw himself into fatherhood when daughter Taylor Nicole Earnhardt was born in December of 1988. "I wasn't around a lot when my other children were growing up," he told the press. "With [Taylor] Nicole, I went through Lamaze classes with Teresa and I was there when she was born. Now that was something. I've seen her grow up. I saw her take her first steps, and I was there when she started talking. I've been here to raise her."

True to her high-octane family, Teresa Earnhardt was never content to rest on her laurels or live off her husband's money. Teresa's business skills always helped ensure that her husband, a man whose early racing endeavors drove him deeply

The 1980s were a successful time for Earnhardt and included a win in the Busch Clash in 1988.

into debt, would never have to borrow money again. It was Teresa who would spearhead Dale Earnhardt, Inc. (DEI), financing racing teams for the Winston Cup and Busch Grand National series, as well as a Chevrolet dealership – all ventures that proved highly successful. After all, what proud car enthusiast wouldn't love to drive an S-10 truck that said "Dale Earnhardt Chevrolet" on it?

She's The Boss

When asked by reporters if he would ever consider leaving Richard Childress Racing to race under his wife at Dale Earnhardt Incorporated, he jokingly replied that "she don't pay too good. So I don't want to drive for her."

With a new lease on life, Earnhardt was ready to start up a new decade and prove to NASCAR fans that he was far more than they had bargained for.

Determination

The longtime partnership between Richard Childress Racing and Wrangler Jeans had been a great one for both sides. But in 1988, it finally came to an end when the contract ran out – leaving Earnhardt in need

Dale Earnhardt, a devoted family man, receives a kiss
from daughter Taylor Nicole after the Busch Clash.

of a new sponsor. Luckily, GM Goodwrench was looking to sponsor a driver and they would come to be Earnhardt's primary sponsor until his death in 2001.

After two seasons of just missing the Winston Cup title, Earnhardt finally began his climb back to the top in 1990. His never-ending quest to win the Daytona 500 continued. He was so close to winning the prestigious race in 1990 that he could smell the champagne – but then a cut tire sent his Lumina flying and dashed his dreams of victory. He would later refer to that race as the "Daytona 499," even though he still managed to take fifth place there, and his impressive record was enough to earn him a fourth Winston Cup title.

Earnhardt and his #3 Chevy were escorted by two mounted policemen when he visited New York City's Central Park in 1990.

The next season brought Earnhardt still more impressive wins, as he rocketed from sixth place to first in one lap during the 1991 Busch Clash sprint race. He would spend the majority of that season in stiff competition with none other than Ricky Rudd, the driver who replaced him on Bud Moore's team when he left to join Richard Childress Racing. After closely beating Rudd and a number of Ford drivers at that year's DieHard 500 at Darlington, he was overheard to quip that he "understood how Custer felt looking at the ridges full of Indians when those Fords lined up to come get me." Earnhardt's considerable skill and the know-how of his pit crew were enough to win him a fifth Cup in 1991.

A Third Generation Takes To The Track

Playing Chicken

For years, a rumor circulated that, at the 1990 Daytona 500, Earnhardt's tires had skidded on a piece of chicken thrown from the stands. Not true – he actually cut his tire on a stray piece of metal.

During the 1992 season, it became clear that Dale and Ralph hadn't been the only Earnhardt boys who wanted to race. Recently out of high school, Dale Jr. went to work for his father's racing organization. Just as Earnhardt's own father had started him out on the smallest jobs, he now went about teaching his own son the ropes from the ground up. He made it clear that Dale Jr. wasn't about to coast into Victory Lane because of his famous name. But it wouldn't be long before "Little E" would prove that he didn't have to, because behind his famous name was a whole lot of talent.

"Black Is Back"

After winning his fifth Winston Cup title in 1991, Earnhardt's performance seemed to slack off during the next year. But The Man In Black's years of experience, both on and off the track, were enough to tell him that setbacks can be overcome. "One thing that has always helped

AP/WWP

Dale Earnhardt Jr. continues the proud racing tradition started by his grandfather Ralph and continued by his father Dale.

The Man In Black shows off plenty of silver after winning race number 70 on March 10, 1996.

me," he told *USA Today* in 1991, "is that I don't dwell on what happened yesterday too much."

A year later, when Richard Childress Racing's press kits carried the slogan "Black Is Back," they meant it. Earnhardt proved he wasn't about to fade away with a stunning victory at the TranSouth 500 at Darlington. By the end of the year, The Intimidator found himself locked in a tight championship race with Mark Martin and Rusty Wallace. The rivalry was enough to make Earnhardt bump Wallace out of the way during the Winston 500, a move that earned him much negative criticism.

But Earnhardt's determination was also enough to win him that sixth Winston Cup.

When the 1994 season ended with Earnhardt taking home a record-tying seventh Winston Cup, it was clear that the combination of Richard Childress Racing and Dale Earnhardt had taken NASCAR racing to a whole new level. But Earnhardt had yet to win the Daytona 500, a prize that would elude him for yet another season.

The Quest For Daytona

Earnhardt would spend three more seasons diligently trying for a Daytona 500 victory. He barely missed it in 1996, the same year he experienced a terrifying wreck at Talladega that left him with a fractured collarbone and sternum – but lucky to be alive. As a result of the crash, Earnhardt suffered from neck and back pain that would continue to plague him for the next two years (until he underwent surgery in 1998.) But even that wreck only kept him off the track for two weeks, proving that The Intimidator certainly was never going to be slowed down by any accident.

The famous Indianapolis Motor Speedway was the site of the 1994 Brickyard 400.

He proved his seeming invincibility again during the next season. When a crash during his run for second place in the Daytona 500 had Earnhardt in the ambulance, he looked over at his damaged Monte Carlo and saw that it still had its tires. When he was told that it would still run, he yelled "Get out of the car!" to the mechanics who were removing it from the field, and took off in it to finish up the race.

Still, a far more frightening incident occurred at Darlington, when Earnhardt temporarily passed out behind the wheel at the Southern 500. Although he was cleared to race again the following weekend, the incident frightened the fans and even The Man In Black himself.

Lucky Charm

After two decades of attempting to win the Daytona 500 – the race that is widely referred to as the NASCAR equivalent of the Super Bowl – without success, it was beginning to look like Earnhardt would never do it. But he proved them all wrong on February 15, 1998, a date that Earnhardt fans everywhere will always remember with the utmost pride.

Teresa helps her husband hoist the 1999 Winston 500 trophy.

The previous day, a group of terminally ill children from the Make A Wish Foundation had visited Earnhardt and one little girl gave him a penny, telling him it was a lucky coin that would help him win the big race.. True to form, Earnhardt glued that penny to his dashboard the next day.

Sure enough, The Intimidator sped his way past his competitors and into the top spot to win NASCAR's most honored race after years of cut tires and breakdowns. In the process, he put an end to an unlucky streak of losing 59 races in a row, and proved himself yet again. When he celebrated his victory by making impromptu doughnuts in the infield, it became one of the most legendary days in the history of NASCAR.

"Earnhardt's the best there is, and that's why he wins races . . . I don't know how he does it. I watch him in awe."

— Jeff Gordon on Earnhardt

AP/WWP

Earnhardt holds his International Race of Champions trophy in one hand and pats Dale Jr. on the back with his other hand.

And, according to The Intimidator himself, he owed this stunning victory all to that penny on the dash. In fact, when his winning car was put on display at Daytona USA, Earnhardt was reportedly upset that he wasn't allowed to keep his penny, the gift from a little girl who believed in him.

Long-Term Memory

When Earnhardt spun driver Rusty Wallace off of the track at Bristol in 1995, Wallace was mad enough to whack Earnhardt over the head with a water bottle, exclaiming, "I ain't forgotten about Talladega [in 1993] either!"

No Checkered Flag

With seven Winston Cups and a Daytona victory under his belt, it looked like The Man In Black had beaten the odds again. But some speculated that it was time for him to hang up his helmet and maybe go into managing Dale Jr.'s budding career instead.

Earnhardt quickly put an end to those rumors. He had put his heart and soul into a racing career, and wasn't about to give up any time soon. "I'm not thinking about retirement by any means," Earnhardt said after winning his 74th Winston Cup race at the 1999 Winston 500.

And he continued to prove his mettle as if he'd never won a thing, zooming to first place in the Winston 500 in 2000. "We're going to win that eighth championship, that's our #1 goal," Richard Childress said in 1999. "Dale Earnhardt can still do it and anyone that's ever doubted it made a big mistake." And Earnhardt never stopped dreaming of that eighth championship.

Earnhardt's success behind the wheel was the result of his skill, but he also used a little luck now and then.

Passing On The Legacy

But Earnhardt never let his success get in the way of mentoring both of his sons. After spending some time driving in the Busch Series, Dale Jr. joined the Winston Cup competition full-time in 2000. Thus, the

Earnhardts joined the honorable tradition of the Pettys, as father and son competed against each other. And competition there definitely was, as Dale Jr. learned when his father actually bumped him out of the way during a 1999 race.

Earnhardt was still going strong when Dale Jr. joined him on the Winston Cup circuit in 1999.

Course Clown

It might seem that a dedicated driver like Earnhardt would have no time for anything that wasn't behind the wheel of his car. But The Man In Black had a genuinely playful side too, one that was rarely seen by anyone outside his close circle of friends. No matter how serious he may have seemed behind the wheel, he still remained the good-hearted practical joker who once left a tin of sardines in Rusty Wallace's car – which Wallace didn't discover until his car began to heat up and fill with the stench!

The Meter's Running

Earnhardt's taste in movies may have run more to *Cool Hand Luke*, but he broke character in 1998 to appear in *BASEketball*. The zany flick starred The Man In Black in a cameo as – of all things – a cab driver.

A Passion For The Great Outdoors

In the rural South where Earnhardt spent his boyhood, hunting and fishing are practically a way of life. And Earnhardt never gave up his boyhood joy of the outdoors. Only now, in his fame, he could afford to fish with a yacht and hunt with much better equipment!

Even in his fishing, he was as competitive as he was on the track. His longtime friend Idus Brendle talked about fishing with Earnhardt: "I remember one day Dale caught a big one . . . . [H]e laid it out on the boat, knowing it would be the biggest one. Next thing you know, I got one that is bigger, and Dale sees that and starts swinging at it with his fishing pole, trying to knock it off. So he's whacking at my fishing pole. Finally, he got my fish off the line, so he still had the biggest fish of the day. The next day at the track, he had people come up to me and ask who had the biggest, because he knew it would get me. You just couldn't catch a bigger fish than him. He wouldn't let you beat him."

Jim Gund/Allsport

Earnhardt had been known to take off his sunglasses and flash a brilliant smile now and then.

Also an avid hunter, Earnhardt traveled all over the country in search of wild game. And yet he kept a small herd of deer on his Mooresville farm and reportedly broke the hand of a local man who tried to shoot one.

The Softer Side Of The Intimidator

To the public, Earnhardt showed his serious side – that of a plank-faced soldier determined to prevail over his opponents no matter what the cost and drive as fast and hard as he could.

Earnhardt was a fan of the Atlanta Braves – and a friend to coach Ned Yost.

Craig Melvin/Allsport

But those lucky enough to call him a friend remember a genuinely soft-hearted man whose compassion knew no bounds. Mooresville still remembers the time that he donated literally tons of seed to help out local farmers after a damaging flood. A lifelong baseball fan and good friend of Atlanta Braves coach Ned Yost, Earnhardt brought baseball to NASCAR country when he sponsored a minor league team in Kannapolis called – appropriately – The Intimidators. Some Alabama motorists still remember the day that Earnhardt, disguised as a state trooper, pulled them over for *not* speeding, and awarded safe drivers with tickets to Talladega.

But Earnhardt had an image to maintain. It would have been difficult for anyone to associate the tough-as-nails driver with the man who could be seen pushing a cart through the Mooresville grocery store like everyone else. Or the man who once walked into a hardware store because he had accidentally run over his youngest daughter's sled and needed the right tools to fix it.

Above all, Earnhardt was known as the man who never forgot where he came from. Despite all the victories, all the fame and all the money, Earnhardt never forgot his roots and never stopped being the good old boy

Intimidating Pasta

Although Earnhardt's favorite food was steak, he had a soft spot for fettuccine alfredo, too. He even asked his friend, California chef Andy Scopazzi, to make it in the pits for him once!

from Kannapolis that he had always been. In the words of *Mooresville Tribune* editor Dale Gowing, The Man In Black was "a regular guy that happened to be a stock car racer, something that a lot of regular guys dream of."

Final Words

It's ultimately tragic that Dale Earnhardt's final race ended with the closing laps of the Daytona 500, the race that he had tried so hard to win for so long was to be his accidental undoing.

But, to be honest, NASCAR's most determined driver probably wouldn't have wanted to go out any other way.

Earnhardt takes a seat on a stack of tires
at Las Vegas Motor Speedway.

www.sportsdesign.com

AP/WWP

Dark Day At Daytona

February 18, 2001

I t was a month before the Daytona 500 and Dale Earnhardt Jr. already knew who was going to win. Fresh out of his rookie NASCAR season, and yearning for a major victory, Dale Jr. told the media that, in a dream he had recently, he was the first driver to cross the finish line at Daytona. "It was so real," he said, "I had to remind myself where I was at." When

Dale Earnhardt could often be found alongside his talented son, Dale Earnhardt Jr.

asked where his father had finished in the race, Dale Jr. replied, "He wasn't there."

Fortunately, young Earnhardt did not know what the future held for his family, for the racing community and for fans of the sport. When he discovered that his father was not at the finish line at Daytona, Dale Jr.'s dream would turn into a nightmare.

Live From Trackside

A few days before Sunday's big race, Dale Earnhardt Sr. was providing some of the entertainment for the crowd at one of the Daytona Speedweeks racing events.

During an IROC series race on Friday, he was forced into the infield grass by fellow racer Eddie Cheever and spun out of contention. But the elder Earnhardt loved the action. "IROC racing is supposed to be fun," he said.

Earnhardt had always showed how much fun he had racing – whether it was the time he spent on the track or celebrating in Victory Lane. But he was not happy with some of the things that were starting to affect the sport he loved. A series of rule changes were slowing down the cars, but were also providing for more exciting races. Although Earnhardt did not like the slower speeds, he was aware that it would help make racing more media-friendly, with frequent lane and lead changes.

Under a newly signed six-year, $2 billion contract, FOX television was scheduled to begin televising NASCAR races, with the 2001 Daytona 500 as its inaugural event. But racing purists were concerned about the quality of race day coverage and analysis.

FOX assured fans that the men behind the microphones would be people that they recognized. Former Winston Cup crew chief Larry McReynolds and Mike Joy, a former CBS racing analyst would be there. As would Darrell Waltrip, the 1989 Daytona champ and brother of Michael Waltrip, the newest member of Earnhardt's Dale Earnhardt Incorporated racing team. What more could Earnhardt's fans ask for?

With NASCAR's new television contract, Dale Earnhardt was primed to drive into the homes of millions of viewers each week.

A New Breed Of Fans

Just as the face of NASCAR was beginning to change due to more extensive television coverage, the faces of the NASCAR fans were also beginning to change. If you looked into the teeming crowds that filled the sold-out Daytona grandstands that Sunday, you would have seen fans representing every walk of life. The appeal of NASCAR had started to cross over to all types of boundaries, bringing all types of people together for the thrill of the sport.

A Dale Earnhardt Jr. fan leaves him a message on the Daytona starting line.

If you happened to be one of those fans who came to the tracks of Daytona on Sunday, February 18, or watched the race from the comfort of your own living room – this is a day that will stay with you for a lifetime, one that you will often hope is just a dream. And while there is little comfort to take regarding the events, you will know that Earnhardt died doing what he loved – driving his black #3 Chevy Monte Carlo.

It Began Like Any Other Race Day . . .

After spending his morning relaxing trackside with his wife, Earnhardt attended a meeting with the other drivers and NASCAR president Mike Helton. Excitement was in the air – a new era in racing was dawning, Helton told the group before him. Expanded television coverage would bring the sport to more Americans than ever before. This was truly going to be a great event.

Soon, the cars lined up at the start. With Jeff Burton beside him, Earnhardt started seventh, on the inside of the fourth row. Sitting in the pole position was Bill Elliott, with Dale Jr. starting sixth and Waltrip behind him, starting 19th. The drivers sat and waited, revving their engines, anticipating the three hours of fierce, competitive driving ahead of them.

A Prayer For Wisdom

For over 10 years, one of the last people to speak to Earnhardt before each race was the Rev. Max Helton (no relation to Mike Helton). As the founder of Motor Racing Outreach, a ministry that has provided spiritual guidance and support to the drivers and their families, Helton stops and says a prayer with many of them before the beginning of each race.

Sunday was no exception. As Earnhardt sat in his car on the track, Helton joined Earnhardt's wife Teresa and car owner Richard Childress and they all "held hands through his window," according to Rev. Helton. Earnhardt then asked Helton to "just pray that I'll be wise in putting the car at the right place at the right time . . . and be able to drive with wisdom." Afterwards, Earnhardt squeezed Helton's hand, "as he always did," recalled Helton, but this time Earnhardt held the squeeze "a little longer then he normally does."

Max Helton prays with Dale Earnhardt Jr. prior to the Dura Lube 400. It was Dale Jr.'s first race after his father's death.

The Green Flag

Earnhardt was correct about the new excitement that he anticipated at Daytona. The race was a thriller from the very beginning. Drivers battled bumper to bumper. Leads changed repeatedly. A quarter of the way into the race, Earnhardt had battled up to the front of the pack. Passing Sterling Marlin, Earnhardt took the lead and remained there for the next 10 laps. Then, Mike Skinner snatched the lead from him, and by Lap 50 Earnhardt was running a solid fourth.

AP/WWP

The amazing efforts of Dale Earnhardt's pit crew often kept
the #3 Chevrolet in the running for a victory.

After a pit stop, Earnhardt fought to regain his place in the pack as he bumped and bullied his way through the mass of cars. First Mark Martin, then Ken Schrader, then Jeff Gordon – they all eventually saw Earnhardt's tail end in front of them. By lap 162, Earnhardt was following his son, but during lap 167, Michael Waltrip passed them both.

Stewart's Flying Machine

With only 26 laps to go, all hell broke loose. With the pack moving at about 180 miles per hour, and in such a tight formation, the inevitable happened. A car got bumped, another car started to spin and it hit the

Pontiac driven by Tony Stewart. Chaos ensued as Stewart's car went airborne. It flip-flopped end-over-end a couple of times and Bobby Labonte ended up on the receiving end of Stewart's flying car. "It's not very much fun when you see a 3,400-pound car fixin' to land on your head," Labonte said after the race.

Tony Stewart (#20) pinwheels across the track after being hit by Robby Gordon (#4). Dale Earnhardt (#3) avoided this crash.

In the end, Stewart was taken to the hospital but later released. Over a dozen drivers were eliminated from the race because of damage to their cars. Finally, the red flag went down, the green flag went up, and the race resumed. Earnhardt driver Steve Park was involved in the smash-up and was out of the race, but the Earnhardts and Waltrip pressed on, down to the final lap. The DEI team was headed for the checkered flag.

In A Blink

All eyes were on the two leaders going down the final stretch. Waltrip, who had taken the lead 15 laps before, was running ahead of Dale Jr. – and they were only seconds from the finish line. Closely following them was Earnhardt. Battling for third place, Earnhardt's car touched Sterling Marlin's Dodge. Earnhardt's #3 suddenly fishtailed, nosed down and slid toward the track's apron. In the blink of an eye, the car jerked to the right and cut across the path of oncoming cars, colliding with Ken Schrader's yellow Pontiac. The two cars hit the upper wall and Earnhardt's car went sliding into the infield grass.

The Best & The Worst

Up in the announcer's booth, a deliriously happy Darrell Waltrip was cheering his brother's victory. As Michael Waltrip took the checkered flag, television audiences cheered along with his brother, "You got it! You got it! Mikeeeeyyyy!" Understandably, Waltrip was anticipating a wild celebration with Michael down in Victory Lane. But the veteran driver's revelry was interrupted when he was abruptly reminded of the cars that did not make it to the finish line.

Dale Earnhardt's tragic crash in the final lap at Daytona left witnesses speechless.

"How about Dale, is he OK?" asked Larry McReynolds, who was with Waltrip in the announcer booth. Waltrip then reacted quickly. "I just hope Dale's OK," he said, murmuring the phrase on the lips of everyone whose attention was now being turned to the broken cars along the wall.

Suddenly, the severity of a seemingly minor crack-up became apparent as Waltrip's tone turned serious. "TV does not do that (crash) justice," he said after seeing the the video replay of the horrible accident along with the television audience. "That is incredible impact. It throws you forward in the car. Those are the kind of accidents that are absolutely frightening."

This was serious. Earnhardt was in trouble. The crowd at the speedway fell silent as Dale Jr. left the Victory Lane area and sprinted toward his father's car in the infield.

Time Stands Still

After the two cars slid down the embankment and came to a stop, Schrader jumped from his car to check on Earnhardt and motioned for the emergency crew. Daytona Speedway's director of emergency services, Dr. Steve Bohannon, rode in the ambulance heading for Earnhardt. When he arrived, the paramedics and another doctor were already administering oxygen and CPR to Earnhardt, who was still trapped in his seat.

The roof of the car was quickly cut away, Earnhardt was removed and loaded into the ambulance. Dale Jr. jumped in to accompany his father and, in less than five minutes, the trauma team at Halifax Medical Center in Daytona Beach was mobilized in an attempt to perform a miracle.

Ken Schrader (#36) collides with Dale Earnhardt (#3)
in the final lap of the Daytona 500.

A Prayer For Strength

Rev. Helton, the man who prayed with Earnhardt before the race, was on his way to congratulate Michael Waltrip. He didn't think Earnhardt's crash looked that serious – no one did. Within minutes, however, he found himself being escorted to Halifax Medical Center and standing again with Teresa and Childress, only this time, they were praying for strength. "They were still working on him at the time, and I was there with (Teresa and Childress) when the doctors told them 'we've done everything we can do.'" Earnhardt was pronounced dead at 5:16 p.m.

No Hope

According to the preliminary autopsy that was performed the following day, Earnhardt's death was caused by blunt force trauma to his head and neck. He also suffered fractures of the sternum, eight broken ribs on his left side and a broken left ankle. The injuries on the left side of his body may be due to the broken seat belt that was found in his car – the lap belt on his *left* side. With a broken belt in his lap, Earnhardt's body was probably thrown forward into the steering wheel. And, without a full-face helmet to protect his head, his chances for survival plummeted.

A Final Thought

Michael Waltrip, in an emotional tribute to his friend, is comforted by the belief that "in a twinkle of an eye, you're in the presence of the Lord, and that's where I think Dale is." And Dale Jr. expressed solemn confidence that he and his family will "get through this."

AP/WWP

The rest of the racing community and Earnhardt's many fans and admirers may need the strength of the man they lovingly called "Ironhead" in order to accomplish the same.

Dale Earnhardt Jr. exits the hospital after his father was pronounced dead.

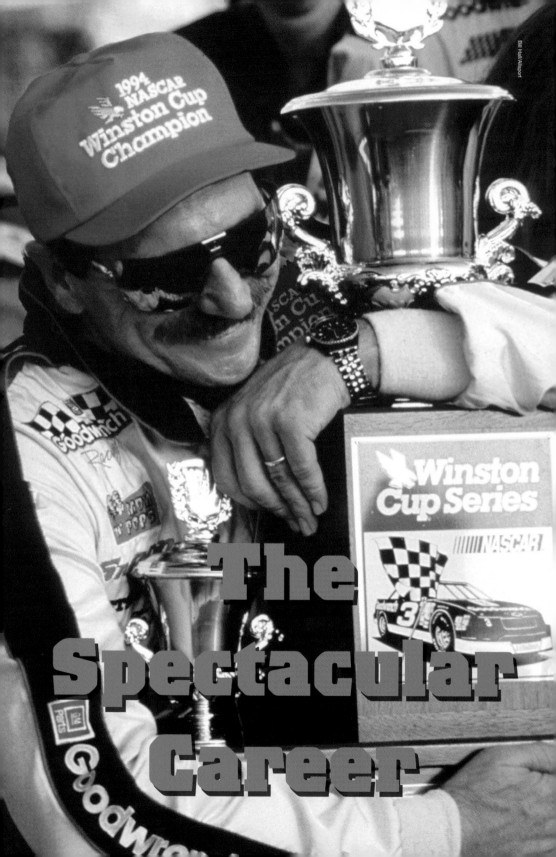

Bill Hall/Allsport

The Spectacular Career

Career Statistics

Dale Earnhardt's career had many highs and lows. Many have said that Earnhardt hungered for glory more than any other Winston Cup driver, and the numbers prove his success.

Year	Starts	Wins	Top 5	Top 10	Winnings	Point Standings
1979	27	1	11	17	$264,086	#7
1980	31	5	19	24	$588,926	#1
1981	31	0	9	17	$347,113	#7
1982	30	1	7	12	$375,325	#12
1983	30	2	9	14	$446,272	#8
1984	30	2	12	22	$616,788	#4
1985	28	4	10	16	$546,596	#8
1986	29	5	16	23	$1,783,880	#1
1987	29	11	21	24	$2,099,243	#1
1988	29	3	13	19	$1,214,089	#3
1989	29	5	14	19	$1,435,730	#2
1990	29	9	18	23	$3,083,056	#1
1991	29	4	14	21	$2,396,685	#1
1992	29	1	6	15	$915,463	#12
1993	30	6	17	21	$3,353,789	#1
1994	31	4	20	25	$3,300,733	#1
1995	31	5	19	23	$3,154,241	#2
1996	31	2	13	17	$2,285,926	#4
1997	32	0	7	16	$2,151,909	#5
1998	33	1	5	13	$2,990,749	#8
1999	34	3	7	21	$2,712,079	#7
2000	34	2	13	24	$4,918,886	#2
2001	1	0	0	0	$296,833	–
Totals	667	76	281	427	$41,278,397	Average: 4.45

Career Wins

I n his career, Dale Earnhardt racked up more than 75 wins, all of which are chronicled here.

1979

April 1 – Southeastern 500

1980

March 16 – Atlanta 500

March 30 – Valleydale
            Southeastern 500

July 12 – Busch Nashville 420

September 28 – Old
               Dominion 500

October 5 – National 500

1982

April 4 – CRC Chemicals
          Rebel 500

1983

July 16 – Busch Nashville 420

July 31 – Talladega 500

1984

July 29 – Talladega 500

November 11 – Atlanta
              Journal 500

1985

February 24 – Miller High
              Life 400

April 6 – Valleydale 500

August 24 – Busch 500

September 22 – Goody's 500

1986

April 13 – TranSouth 500

April 20 – First Union 400

May 25 – Coca-Cola 600

October 5 – Oakwood Homes 500

November 2 – Atlanta Journal 500

1987

March 1 – Goodwrench 500

March 8 – Miller High Life 400

March 29 – TranSouth 500

April 5 – First Union 400

April 12 – Valleydale Meats 500

April 26 – Sovran Bank 500

June 28 – Miller American 400

July 19 – Summer 500

August 22 – Busch 500

September 6 – Southern 500

September 13 – Wrangler Jeans
               Indigo 400

1988

March 20 – Motorcraft Quality
           Parts 500

April 24 – Pannill Sweatshirts 500

August 27 – Busch 500

1989

April 16 – First Union 400

June 4 – Budweiser 500

September 3 – Heinz
            Southern 500
September 17 – Peak
            Performance 500
November 19 – Atlanta
            Journal 500

1990

March 18 – Motorcraft Quality
            Parts 500
April 1 – TranSouth 500
May 6 – Winston 500
June 24 – Miller Genuine
            Draft 400
July 7 – Pepsi 400
July 9 – DieHard 500
September 2 – Heinz
            Southern 500
September 9 – Miller Genuine
            Draft 400
November 4 – Checker 500

1991

February 24 – Pontiac
            Excitement 400
April 28 – Hanes 500
July 28 – DieHard 500
September 29 – Tyson/Holly
            Farms 400

1992

May 24 – Coca-Cola 600

1993

March 28 – TranSouth 500
May 30 – Coca-Cola 600

June 6 – Budweiser 500
July 3 – Pepsi 400
July 18 – Miller Genuine
            Draft 500
July 25 – DieHard 500

1994

March 27 – TranSouth 500
April 10 – Food City 500
May 1 – Winston Select 500
October 23 – ACDelco 500

1995

April 9 – First Union 400
May 7 – Save Mart 300
August 5 – Brickyard 400
September 24 – Goody's 500
November 12 – NAPA 500

1996

February 25 – Goodwrench 400
March 10 – Purolator 500

1998

February 15 – Daytona 500

1999

April 25 – DieHard 500
August 28 – Goody's 500
October 17 – Winston 500

2000

March 12 – Cracker Barrel 500
October 15 – Winston 500

Career Highlights

The Intimidator had a career that other drivers could only dream about. Here a few of the highlights of his more than 20-year run as racing's greatest driver.

1975

• Dale Earnhardt competes in his first Winston Cup race, the World 600, at Charlotte Motor Speedway on May 25, 1975. He came in 22nd.

Pole Position

Earnhardt won his first Winston Cup pole on June 8, 1979 at Riverside Speedway in only his 24th start.

1979

• Earnhardt wins the Winston Cup Rookie of the Year award.

• Earnhardt wins his first Winston Cup race at Bristol Motor Speedway on April 1, 1979.

• By season's end, Earnhardt earns more than $200,000 in purses.

Dale Earnhardt's first victory came in 1979 at Bristol Motor Speedway.

1980

• Earnhardt captures his first Winston Cup championship in his sophomore season. He secures it by finishing fifth in the Los Angeles Times 500 at Ontario Motor Speedway, the last race of the year. By winning this championship, he becomes the first driver ever to win Rookie of the Year and a Winston Cup championship in consecutive years.

• Earnhardt, driving a blue and yellow Chevy for Roy Osterlund, racks up his first superspeedway win in the spring of 1980 when he races to victory in the Atlanta 500. Impressively, he had started that race in the 31st position!

• Earnhardt gets his very first Driver of the Year Award from the National Motorsports Press Association.

Earnhardt's racing helmet and dark sunglasses can't hide the look of determination on his face.

• Earnhardt wins the Busch Clash. He would go on to win this race six times – the only driver to do so.

1984

• Earnhardt wins the DieHard 500 at Talladega, becoming the only driver to win it back-to-back (he also won it in 1983).

1986

• Earnhardt nets his second Winston Cup championship, marking the first time since 1978 that the championship was clinched before the final race of the season.

• Earnhardt's quest for an elusive Daytona 500 victory ends when he runs out of gas only three laps from the finish and Geoff Bodine beats him to the checkered flag.

• Earnhardt wins Driver of the Year again, this time sharing the honor with Tim Richmond.

• Earnhardt adds a second Busch Clash win to his resume.

The Intimidator often left competitors such as Dale Jarrett (blue car) in the dust.

1987

• Earnhardt takes the Winston Select in 1987 with a move that has become legendary – his famous "pass in the grass."

• Earnhardt gets off to a smoking start in '87, winning six of the first eight races of the year – at Rockingham, Richmond, Darlington, North Wilkesboro, Bristol and Martinsville.

• With his aggressive driving and take-no-prisoners attitude, Earnhardt clinches his second straight Winston Cup title earlier than any driver since Cale Yarborough in 1977.

• He's named American Motorsports Driver of the Year and receives the NMPA Driver of the Year award.

1988

• Earnhardt becomes The Man In Black. He has traded in his blue

The pit crew works furiously on Earnhardt's #3 Chevrolet.

Bill Hall/Allsport

and yellow Wrangler car for his now-famous black Monte Carlo, with GM Goodwrench as his official sponsor.

1990

• Earnhardt races to his fourth Winston Cup championship with a 24-point margin.

• Fate manages to ruin yet another Daytona 500, as Earnhardt cuts a tire on the final lap and finishes a disappointing fifth.

• Earnhardt wins two of the three Winston Million events and picks up a $100,000 "consolation" bonus.

• His record earnings for the season top the $3 million mark.

• Earnhardt takes the first of four International Race of Champions series races this year.

• He wins the NMPA Driver of the Year award.

1991

• Earnhardt wins his second consecutive Winston Cup championship (and fifth overall) by a very comfortable 195 points.

A Pretty Penny

In his career as a NASCAR driver, Earnhardt won more than $41,000,000 – the most in NASCAR history!

• Earnhardt wins the DieHard 500 at Talladega, one of his four wins for the year.

• Earnhardt wins the Busch Clash for the fourth time.

• Another bizarre Daytona 500: Earnhardt hits a sea gull at full speed, then collides with Davey Allison late in the race.

1993

• Earnhardt wins the Coca-Cola 600 despite being penalized three laps.

• Earnhardt and Rusty Wallace battle for much of the season, but in the end, The Intimidator wins his sixth Winston Cup championship by 80 points.

Hall Of Famer

Earnhardt will be eligible for induction into the International Motorsports Hall of Fame in 2006.

• With his win at The Winston, Earnhardt becomes the first three-time winner of that race.

• Earnhardt wins his fifth Busch Clash.

AP/WWP

Dale Earnhardt's victories provided him the opportunity to celebrate with famous people including Colin Powell (far left).

Earnhardt acknowledges the crowd after winning the 1995 Brickyard 400 in Indianapolis, Indiana.

1994

• Now with his seventh Winston Cup championship win, Earnhardt ties the legendary driver Richard Petty for the all-time record for Winston Cup championships.

• The year also sees Earnhardt top the $3 million mark in earnings. This is the third time he's accomplished the feat in five years.

1995

• Earnhardt grabs his first road course victory ever, at Sears Point Raceway in Sonoma, California.

1996

• Earnhardt becomes only the third driver ever to start 500 consecutive Winston Cup races.

• Although he again fails to win the Daytona 500 this year, Earnhardt does win the pole position. This marks the ninth time he's accomplished such a feat at that track.

• At The Winston, Earnhardt drives a car with a special paint scheme saluting the Atlanta Olympics.

Jeff Gordon (right) tries unsuccessfully to pass Earnhardt in the 1998 Daytona 500. It was Dale's first Daytona 500 victory in 20 tries.

1997

• The Intimidator becomes the first race car driver to appear on a Wheaties cereal box.

1998

• The Man In Black finally slays the dragon by winning the Daytona 500 on his 20th attempt. After the race, opposing crew members line up to slap Earnhardt's hand and offer congratulations as The Intimidator idles by.

• He finishes in the top 10 in point standings for the 18th time in his career.

• Earnhardt is voted "NASCAR's Greatest Driver" by racing fans.

Victory At Last

When Dale finally won the Daytona 500 in 1998, the victory broke a 59-race winless streak.

1999

• Earnhardt makes his 600th consecutive start on August 15, 1999.

2000

• After starting from the 35th position, Earnhardt roars to a win at the Cracker Barrel 500.

• Earnhardt wins the Winston 500 at Talladega, giving him 10 career victories at the superspeedway. This win would go down in history as his final victory.

• The Intimidator proves he still has what it takes, finishing second in the points race to Bobby Labonte.

Earnhardt celebrates with a crowd of jubilant fans at Talladega.

Jon Ferrey/Allsport

Crown Jewels Of Racing

There is no such thing as an unimportant race in the Winston Cup series. Winning the championship hinges on how well a driver performs week in, week out. The following famous races are regarded by many as the "jewels" in NASCAR's crown. Dale Earnhardt's memorable performances at these tracks ensure his position in stock car royalty.

Brickyard 400

The longtime home of Indy car racing, Indianapolis Motor Speedway was invaded by stock cars in 1994. When the Brickyard 400 was added to the Winston Cup schedule, drivers couldn't wait to

Darkness At Daytona

After Earnhardt's tragic accident at Daytona in 2001, he was credited with a 12th-place finish.

speed over the famous track that was once paved in brick. Earnhardt taught those Indy boys a thing or two about racing when he took the 1995 Brickyard 400.

AP/WWP

The Intimidator celebrates yet another win.

Coca-Cola 600

Originally known as the World 600, this race held at Lowe's Motor Speedway in North Carolina is a true endurance test for drivers. Its 600 miles make it the longest Winston Cup event. Earnhardt has a long history with the track – his first Winston Cup start came in 1975 in the World 600. In those days, the track was still known as Charlotte Motor Speedway, but whatever its name, Earnhardt always raced fearlessly and competitively there.

Daytona 500

The Daytona 500 is NASCAR's most famous race. For many years, it seemed like Earnhardt was cursed at this legendary race. He came close in 1984, 1986, 1990, 1993 and 1996, but was denied entry into Victory Lane each time. This run of bad luck ended in 1998, when Earnhardt finally earned the win that had eluded him for decades.

Southern 500

Held at Darlington Raceway, "The Track Too Tough To Tame," the Southern 500 never scared The Intimidator. Earnhardt stared down the mighty track like an outlaw gunfighter and made it blink three times in his career. Earnhardt set the speed record for the track on March 3, 1993, running his #3 Chevrolet 139.958 miles per hour.

Winston 500

Held late in the season at Talladega (considered the fastest NASCAR track), the Winston 500 has helped decide many Winston Cup championships. The brooms were ready in 1999 when Earnhardt swept both races at Talladega, including the Winston 500. These victories for The Man In Black were sweet revenge after a scary accident at the track in 1996 demolished his #3 Chevrolet.

Earnhardt sweeps away fake money after winning the 2000 Winston 500 in Talladega.

Dale's Tales

Whether you knew him as a family man, a neighbor, a friend or a racing rival, you could appreciate Dale Earnhardt as a person. His 49 years were filled with laughter, good times and emotion, both on and off the track. Here's a glimpse at some stories that show off the wonderful and generous personality that was Dale Earnhardt.

Dale's Dugout Dream

Earnhardt was an avid fan of baseball's Atlanta Braves. As such, he continually pestered good friend and Braves third base coach Ned Yost to let him sit in the dugout during a game. As Yost told *The Atlanta Journal-Constitution*, "Dale was always talking about wanting to sit in our dugout during a game. I told him, 'Sure, go ahead, call [baseball commissioner] Bud Selig for permission.' He'd say 'Well, that's no problem. I'll just call Bud Selig.'

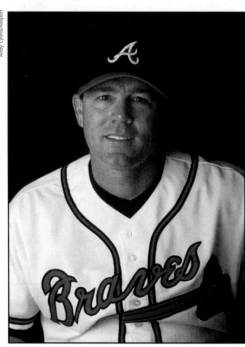

Andy Lyons/Allsport

Ned Yost, third base coach for the Atlanta Braves.

"I told him, 'Dale, you can call him, but it's not going to change anything. You can't sit on the bench during a game. Look, we don't ask to sit in your car when you're driving a race.' And he'd say, 'I'm not asking to stand next to [Greg] Maddux when he's pitching. I just want to sit on the bench, help manage a game.'"

In another incident, Dale was having problems getting his car ready before an Atlanta race. "Call [manager] Bobby [Cox] and see if he has any ideas,"

Dale told Yost. "Bobby has as much an idea about setting up a car as you do about running a pitching staff," was the response that he got.

The Rocking Chair Derby

Earnhardt and racing buddy Darrell Waltrip shared an ongoing joke throughout their years of racing on the Winston Cup circuit together. The two liked to banter about how when they were old and retired, they could sit together in their rocking chairs and reminisce about their racing days. In fact, Dale even presented Waltrip with a rocking chair for his retirement. " There's a place here in North Carolina," Darrell recently said, "that makes these gigantic rocking chairs. I was going to buy one and ship it to [Dale for his retirement], because you know his chair had to be bigger and rock faster."

Darrell Waltrip, in his last year before retirement, pals around with Dale Earnhardt at a 2000 ceremony.

Lucky Penny

As Dale prepared to defend his title as the reigning Daytona 500 champion in 1999, he made sure he had one thing on hand – his lucky penny. After his 1998 win, Dale had glued the penny to the inside of the car, where it had stayed ever since. However, he made sure to retrieve his good luck charm for the 1999 race, threatening his competitors, "I know the date on it. I know the penny, so if somebody has changed it, I'll know." Unfortunately, the penny did not bring success to Dale a second time, but the memories will last forever.

Very Funny . . .

Dale wasn't afraid to put the pedal to the metal on or off the track.

Auto racing reporter Ed Hinton fondly recalls how he learned a hard lesson about driving with The Intimidator. Going approximately 105 miles per hour down a country highway, Dale told Hinton to "hold on."

Before Hinton had a chance to react, "[Dale] throws the pickup into a boot-legger turn, a 180-degree spin at 105 miles an hour, and the entire world goes up in tire smoke, and I'm flung across the cab, all the way across him with my head hanging out the driver's-side window by the time we come to a stop. He shoves me hard – 'Git offa me! I tol' you to hold on!' I gather myself and I am raging, livid, the first cuss words on the tip of my tongue and I look at him and he is grinning. 'Next time I tell you to 'hold on,' I bet you'll do it."

Late Night With David Letterman

After his 1998 Daytona win, Dale himself even took part in the barbs about his lengthy struggle to capture the victory. In one particularly memorable appearance, he was a guest on *Late Night With David Letterman.* But rather than being interviewed, Dale was there to read that night's Top Ten list – "Top Ten Reasons It Took Me 20 Years To Win The Daytona 500." Listed are the responses:

David Letterman invited Dale on his show after his victory in the Daytona 500.

10. It took me 19 years to realize I had the emergency brake on.

9. Finally rotated and balanced my moustache.

8. Quit training with the Canadian snowboarding team.

7. Stopped letting my 300-pound cousin, Ricky, ride shotgun.

6. New strategy: pretend I'm Dave driving home on the Merritt Parkway.

5. Who cares that it took me 20 years – at least my name isn't Dick Trickle.

4. Just figured out that if you mash the gas pedal all the way down, the car takes off like a son-of-a-b****.

3. My new pit crew – The Spice Girls.

2. This year, whenever I'd pass somebody, I'd give them the finger.

1. My secret to success: one can of motor oil in my engine, one can of motor oil in my pants.

. . . But He Doesn't Always Play The Part

Dale may be a force to be reckoned with on the track, but off the track he's got a sensitive side that shines through. Chip Williams, a former NASCAR public relations specialist told this story of the racing legend to *The Atlanta Journal-Constitution*. "Back in 1990, I had gotten a letter from a 15-year-old kid who was dying of cancer. He wanted to meet Dale Earnhardt. I took the letter to Dale at Talladega the following week. He called the kid at the hospital and talked to him for about 15 minutes. I thought it was a pretty cool thing for Earnhardt to do. I told some reporters about it, and they wanted to interview Dale. He got so mad. I told him, 'It would be good publicity and good for your image.' He said, 'I don't want to talk about it. I didn't do it for the publicity. And I don't want that kid to think that was the reason I called.' I felt like dirt after Earnhardt said that. He could make a lot of people mad on a race track, but he made up for it a thousand times off the race track. People will just never know."

Dr. Earnhardt

After a mysterious blackout at the August 1997 Southern 500 at the Darlington Raceway, Dale had 16 doctors examining him to try to figure

out what had gone wrong and caused this. "They didn't check to see if I was pregnant," Earnhardt wisecracked to *Sports Illustrated*, "but they did everything else. And they didn't find anything." When a series of tests on the heart and the brain proved inconclusive, Earnhardt gave his own diagnosis of what happened that day: a bad tomato.

Was it a combination like this that caused Earnhardt's "goofiness" on the track?

"I ate a whole fresh tomato with my lunch and drank two glasses of a sports drink that opens the pores in your stomach, allowing it to take more fluid in. I took three Actrons, which I have taken before a lot of races because it relaxes your muscles and you don't cramp. I think the combination of the tomato, the sports drink and the Actron reacted on me chemically and caused what happened. It was like somebody shot a bullet in my arm and I went goofy," the driver later told a reporter.

Earnhardt's theory has since become a running joke between skeptical doctors, but he always made sure to avoid the combination before races after that incident, and never had another similar scare.

Tractor-Racing On The Tonight Show

When Dale Earnhardt appeared on *The Tonight Show With Jay Leno* in September of 1995, it marked the first time that a Winston Cup racer had ever been on the late-night talk show.

Leno, a classic car enthusiast, is a fan of auto racing (and in recent years has even had the honor of driving the Indy pace car, which had absolutely thrilled him).

One of the highlights of the broadcast was when Jay challenged Dale to a tractor race. Jay won – but he also admits that he made an illegal cut across the field to cut off The Intimidator.

Car buff Jay Leno got behind the wheel of a tractor to race Dale on *The Tonight Show.*

Why He's Called The Intimidator

Dale Earnhardt had earned his nickname, The Intimidator. He was known throughout the racing circuit as a brash personality who was fierce both on and off the track. He wasn't afraid of anything, especially taking

Jim Gund/ICON SMI

The crew works hard to keep the car up to speed – obviously doing a good job as after a spectacular crash, the car still started.

risks. An example of Earnhardt's perseverance came in the 1997 Daytona 500 when he suffered a terrible wreck, rolling his car a few times. As Earnhardt was loaded into an ambulance, he turned to the driver of the wrecker that was sent to take his car off the track and asked if it would start. The driver said that it had indeed started. "Get out, I've got to go," Earnhardt announced, marching back into his car to complete the race.

Defeating Daytona

After a frustrating 19 losses at the Daytona 500 during his Winston Cup career, Dale Earnhardt revved up his engine and headed out onto the Daytona International Speedway again on February 15, 1998. This time the outcome would be different. After 200 laps, the seven-time Winston Cup champion pulled into Victory Lane, while much of the race's 180,000 spectator audience gave The Intimidator a standing ovation and pit crew members from virtually every team raced to congratulate him.

And it was an emotional victory for Earnhardt as well. In fact, he initially admitted that upon realizing that he was winning, he cried. But soon after, he told reporters, "I don't think I really cried. My eyes watered up."

So through his watering eyes, Earnhardt celebrated the event by immediately cutting a series of doughnuts in the grass to form a #3. Proud of his artistic talent, Earnhardt pointed his second accomplishment of the day to out to his viewers in the pressroom, "I'm pretty good at writin', huh?"

Later that evening, Earnhardt remained in good spirits as he joked around with press members. Arriving at the conference, he pulled a stuffed monkey from behind his back and threw it into the audience. "I'm here," he announced to the crowd, "And I've got that g****** monkey off my back!"

. . . And A "Good Ol' Boy" Until The End

Until his untimely death, Dale Earnhardt was one of the few "good ol' boys" left in the sport of auto racing. Not there for the money or the recognition, Dale raced for the sheer enjoyment of the sport. He grew up surrounded by the sport (his father Ralph was one of the original stock car racers) and remained passionate about it until the very end. And that is what NASCAR is truly all about.

Dale prepares to win his first
Daytona 500 on February 15, 1998.

The Danger Zone

Dale Earnhardt®
Close Calls

The wold of racing is full of excitement, but that excitement does not come without its costs. In such a fast-paced sport, there are sure to be spills as well as thrills in every race. And for Earnhardt, these spills were all just part of a typical day at work.

July 30, 1979 – Coca-Cola 500
Pocono International Raceway

Earnhardt's stellar rookie year of 1979, which had included 17 top 10 finishes and the Rookie of the Year award, was marred by a major collision while racing at Pocono on July 30th.

Earnhardt was leading the race when he blew a tire and got into a violent crash. Among his many painful injuries from the wreck were two broken collarbones, severe bruising and a concussion. Earnhardt was very fortunate to be able to walk away from the terrible crash with just these injuries. But in true Earnhardt style, the worst part for him was not the pain, but missing four races. "I was on top of the world," Earnhardt said, "and then, just like that, I was back listening to races on the radio."

The damage done to Earnhardt's door is clear to see in this photo from 2000.

Earnhardt was temporarily replaced by substitute David Pearson, which was a source of consternation for the young Intimidator. When a little over a month later, Pearson rode Earnhardt's Osterlund Chevrolet to victory at the Southern 500 at Darlington, Earnhardt remembered the substitute win with pleasure. "I was proud to have him in that car. It showed the class of the team we had at that time." Incidentally, that was to be the very last race weekend that Earnhardt spent outside of his race car.

July 25, 1982 – Mountain Dew 500 Pocono International Raceway

Another dangerous crash came three years later at the Mountain Dew 500. This time, it wasn't a tire, but failed brakes that sent Earnhardt into a collision. Earnhardt smashed into Tim Richmond in the first turn, sending both cars into the wall.

Earnhardt walks away almost completely unscathed form his overturned car in 1982.

And then Earnhardt's car flipped over: "I lost the brakes going into the turn," he explained. "I kept pumping but there wasn't anything there. I then hit Richmond and we both took a wild ride." Richmond's description made it sound more fun than it probably was: "Dale's car spun and hit me and we were off to the races."

Robby Gordon (#13), Bobby Labonte (#18), Tony Stewart (#20) and Jeremy Mayfield (#12) avoid Earnhardt's spinning car during a race in 2000.

The force of the collision against the thick, boiler plate wall practically demolished Earnhardt's car, but miraculously, Earnhardt and Richmond suffered only minor injuries. When Earnhardt was released from the hospital, team owner Bud Moore said to his young driver, "You're not going to believe that car," referring to his astonishment that Earnhardt crawled out of the wreck with few physical injuries. They were both very lucky, as Earnhardt explained, "When you have a wreck at Pocono, you really hit hard."

May 17, 1987 – The Winston Charlotte Motor Speedway

The infamous "pass in the grass" during the last several laps of 1987's Winston is among the most memorable at the Charlotte Motor Speedway and confirms that Earnhardt was nothing less than a racing superhero. On the last leg of the grueling race, Earnhardt, Bill Elliott and Geoff Bodine raced hard and furious for the lead, often bumping each other and even sending Bodine into a spin.

Then, with Earnhardt approaching Elliott to snag first place, Earnhardt's car was pushed onto the grass. Without spinning out – as a car usually would when it changes surfaces quickly and traveling upwards of 200 miles an hour – Earnhardt passed Elliott and some contend that he nudged Elliott into the wall, sustaining the lead to win the race.

Furious for having the Winston "stolen" from him, Elliott located Earnhardt's car on the track during the cool-down lap and drove into him. Bodine followed Elliott's lead and also rammed Earnhardt.

Elliott insisted, "If a man has to run over you to beat you, it's time to stop." Earnhardt felt quite differently, asserting that, "Bill got me sideways and knocked me into the grass. . . . I never touched the man in turn four." However when referring to the incident, Earnhardt stated that the decision of who was at fault was " . . . a deal between me and Bill and no one else." However, NASCAR saw it differently and fined all three drivers – Earnhardt, Elliott and Bodine.

July 28, 1996 – DieHard 500 Talladega Superspeedway

Earnhardt got off to one of his best starts, leading the race at the DieHard 500 in 1996 before he crashed. When battling Sterling Marlin for the lead with Ernie Irvan hot on their tail, Irvan's car bumped Marlin's and sent Marlin into Earnhardt. Earnhardt's car careened into the wall, tumbled over, finally landing on its side where it was struck by other cars. The pileup took out several other cars.

Earnhardt had to be cut out of his car, but he walked to an ambulance under his own power with a broken collarbone and breastbone. He was held overnight and released the next day. "I feel very fortunate," Earnhardt said at the time. "It is a situation like this that makes one appreciate the high safety standards required by NASCAR."

Lowe's Motor Speedway president Humpy Wheeler remarked, "The thing we always fear is, what if a driver gets hit with his car upside down?

And this one ended up on its side, and no one could survive the kind of wreck he had . . . The fact that he walked out of that car is phenomenal." While Earnhardt did walk away from the crash, he would suffer chronic neck problems over the next few years that would eventually end after his surgery in 1999.

February 16 – 1997 Daytona 500
Daytona International Speedway

His arch nemesis, the Daytona 500 would get the better of Earnhardt again in 1997. With a few laps to go and only Bill Elliott in the way of Earnhardt's trip to Victory Lane, the #3 jolted to the left after being passed closely by Jeff Gordon, hitting the wall and grazing Gordon before he was hit by an oncoming car driven by Dale Jarrett. Earnhardt was propelled into the air and Ernie Irvan's car became Earnhardt's cushion as he sailed down on top of it, sending Irvan's hood flying into the stands. The Intimidator landed back on the track, spun and eventually came to a halt.

The ambulance crew wanted to take him to the hospital to check for bumps and bruises, but upon seeing that his mangled car still had all its tires inflated and that the engine started, The Man In Black hopped back into the driver's seat to finish the race. "I just wanted to get back in the race, try to make laps," said Earnhardt, who drove the taped-up, mangled hunk of sheet metal across the finish line, for a disappointing 31st-place finish.

On the backstretch, Earnhardt flips upside down in front of Ernie Irvan (#28) in this 1997 photo.

Gordon, who was slightly concerned that The Man In Black would take out any residual anger for his crash when they both returned to the garage, was surprised to catch a glimpse of a smiling Earnhardt giving him the thumbs-up sign.

August 31, 1997 – The Mountain Dew Southern 500 Darlington Raceway

After having an episode similar to a migraine where blood supply to the brain is restricted, Earnhardt started the only race he swears he can't remember. Twice before the race, Earnhardt nodded off at the wheel and as soon as the race started, Earnhardt barreled into the wall on turn one and again at turn two. Car owner Richard Childress radioed Earnhardt to pit but he drove right past the entrance and had to circle around again. Earnhardt was pulled, limp, out of his car. "About two minutes before the race started, a couple of us commented that he didn't look the same," said a member of Earnhardt's team of the confusing incident. Although not among his more mangled crashes, the dizzy spell had Earnhardt reevaluating his ability to continue racing and wondering if he'd ever get behind the wheel again. Luckily for fans everywhere, he was back behind the wheel in record time.

Earnhardt goes head-to-head with both Jeff Gordon and Steve Park at Lowe's Motor Speedway in May 2000.

Life Behind The Wheel

Stock car racing is an endurance sport and a game of strategy all wrapped up into one exciting package. Drivers must be up for the challenge of driving 500 miles around the same track for hours – and they're not going for the traditional Sunday drive, either! With speeds that can be clocked at more than 200 mph and the heat cranked up to blistering inside the cockpit, there's no room for error, fatigue or even the slightest bit of hesitation.

Casey Atwood's team prepares his #19 Dodge at Daytona International Speedway.

Suiting Up

You have to be mentally prepared for race day, and the comfort of a regular routine goes a long way in easing the pre-race jitters. While your team is hard at work making last-minute adjustments to your car following the practice run, you suit up in your fireproof uniform, full-face helmet, driving gloves and specialized shoes.

Getting In And Starting The Engine

You're suited up, the car is ready and now the race is about to begin. You're ready to get into the driver's seat, but you can't just open the door, because your car doesn't have any door handles. Actually, it doesn't even have any doors! How are you going to get in? Hopefully, you're agile enough to slip in through the window, because that's the only way!

As you slide into the driver's seat, you'll notice that it is perfectly formed to your body. In order to prevent neck and back injuries, seats are cast to the driver's frame to ensure that there's no room for jostling about at the wheel. Just in case you find yourself spinning on the track, the mere shape of your seat will help keep you in place and you'll be better able to steer yourself to safety.

Let's Get Ready To Race!

For the longer-endurance races on the circuit, you must be able to pace yourself. Sure, you've got a rumbling powerhouse underneath you, but it's also a delicate machine that, if it's run too hard and for too long, could very easily stop performing.

It's not his usual Monte Carlo, but Dale Earnhardt has no trouble easing behind the wheel of this Corvette.

Tires are also key to a driver's performance on the track. Each tire is filled and treated differently depending on the characteristics of each and every racetrack. A blown tire can, at the very least, take you down a few laps, and at the most, cause a run-in with another driver, a spinout or a bump against the wall that will destroy the aerodynamics of your car. And, in worse case scenarios, tire problems, if they're severe enough, can even take you out of the race entirely.

See The Spotter Run

Your car also does not have any mirrors, so you can't see behind you, but even if you could, your helmet and neck supports make your side vision almost useless. So now what? How can you pass and bump your competitors without knowing who's around you? Now would be a good time for you to turn on your headset.

Well-timed pit stops are often the difference between victory and defeat.

Throughout the race, you'll be in direct radio contact with a teammate called a spotter. He (or she) is perched on top of your team's trailer in the infield and his job is to watch every piece of action on the track. He'll maintain continuous contact with you, keeping you aware of your competitors and who's behind and next to you on the track. He'll also suggest strategies to help you overtake your opponents.

Spotters also keep an eye out for any wear to the tires or car. They know how much a tire can take, and they communicate constantly with their drivers. They work together to develop strategies for pit stops, including when it's the best time for a driver to come down pit road and how much service the car should get.

Suck It Up!

Drivers can lose as much as 5 to 10 pounds during a race due to perspiration. So, tightening the seat belt regularly is a good idea!

If you think your tires are holding up fine, and you're not feeling any reluctance in your brakes, but your fuel is running low, you'll want to tell your spotter that you'll be coming in for a "gas and go."

You Can Taste The Victory

Now the race is well under way and nearing the final laps, but you find yourself running in third place during the last two laps. Your car is still handling fine, and you put four new tires on during your last pit stop and didn't lose any time. It's time for some strategizing.

With your hands hot on the steering wheel, you feel secure that you can pass the second-place car on the next turn. He's been running high on the turns all afternoon and if your spotter says "Clear low!" you'll sneak past him on the low side of the track the second you get close enough. You have a teammate behind you, and even though he badly wants to take the checkered flag for himself, you know he'll ward off any oncoming traffic for you and aid you in your maneuver.

Say What?

Your spotter may tell you "You're running three wide," (meaning you are one of three cars racing side by side) or "Clear high!" (meaning it is clear to pass on the high side of the track).

Congratulations! You completed the move successfully, and with second place secured, your spotter, crew and fans are cheering you on to

AP/WWP

Dale Earnhardt attempts to pass race leader
Jeff Gordon at the 1999 Daytona 500.

the finish. The race leader – who hasn't been handling well in the last few laps and didn't pit for gas just so he could gain a few-second lead – is probably sweating, knowing that you're so close and are actively eyeing his position.

If you're up for the Earnhardt style of offensive driving, you'll sneak up close to the leader, and accelerate until you're both side by side. Giving it your all, you wedge yourself close so that the other driver is forced to the high side of the track, slowing his momentum.

Mission accomplished! You've nudged the leader out of the way and the checkered flag belongs to you! Now you are running your victory lap

with the track empty and open in front of you. Fans are cheering and you know your family and team-mates are waiting for you!

Pop The Cork!

Victory has never been sweeter! Climb on top of your car! The crew will bang out those footprint dents later, but right now, with flashes going off

Dale Earnhardt gives Andy Pilgrim a champagne shower after the Rolex 24 in Daytona Beach.

every second and microphones thrust in your face, you've got your crew to thank and sponsors to please. Give that champagne bottle a shake and celebrate!

Keeping It Safe

If you think stock car racing looks like a dangerous sport now, you should have seen it in the old days. After a half-century of NASCAR racing, many safety regulations have been enhanced. Although accidents still tragically occur and fans and NASCAR officials often push to change safety standards, the sport is a lot safer than it was for NASCAR's originators. Car modifications, new rules and personal equipment have saved many a driver from serious injuries.

The Car – Showroom To Space-Age

If you've ever seen a Chevrolet Monte Carlo on the road or at the dealership, you'll notice that it looks nothing like the models that carried The Intimidator to victory lane so often. When a NASCAR driver gets involved with the world of racing, he has to qualify his car, and that

means rebuilding a standard-model car practically from the ground up. Those long and weary hours pay off by making the car a vehicle suited for traveling at 180 mph and allowing the driver to live to tell about it.

Shattered glass in a car accident can cause serious damage to anyone inside, so stock cars

Stock cars are equipped with protective window nets and plastic windshields to prevent injury.

today are built with no glass at all. The front and rear windshields are made of hard plastic – called Lexan – that doesn't shatter. Cars have a Lexan window on the passenger side for the longer tracks and no passenger side window for the shorter ones. The driver's side has a net over the open window to keep him inside, should the car become airborne.

Although there are no doors on the car, Dale Earnhardt Jr. can chat with his father through its window.

Incidentally, those nets can help a driver communicate in case an accident does happen. If the driver is able to unhook the net from the window, that action lets the rescue team know that he's all right. That window is the only way in or out of the car, since it doesn't have any doors, either.

Strapped In

Consider the speed attained by NASCAR drivers, and you'll know that just one standard seat belt isn't enough. To keep in one place while driving, a NASCAR driver will use five seat belts at once! A belt comes around the waist from each side (the one on Earnhardt's left side is the one that came unsecured during his fatal Daytona 500 accident), another goes diagonally over each shoulder and one goes up between his knees, with one big buckle in the middle to hold it all together. The buckle is similar to the one in your own car, which makes the whole apparatus easy to get out of, but invaluable in keeping a driver in one place.

Stop, Drop And Roll

The last thing a driver wants during a race is to have a fire. In the early days of the Daytona dirt tracks, fire hazards were an issue, but that changed when fuel tanks were fitted with interior rubber bladders. If one car rams another in the gas tank, a rubber cell keeps the tank from exploding. Just to be extra careful, every car has a fire extinguisher in an easily accessible location.

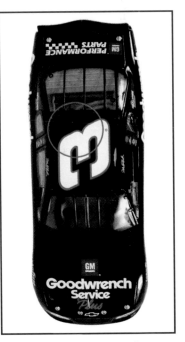

Roof flaps prevent stock cars from lifting off the track.

Staying Grounded

AP/WWP

Dale Earnhardt's fire-retardant suit also shows off his many sponsors.

If you look carefully at a stock car, you'll see small flaps in the roof. They may look like they're meant for ventilation, but their real purpose is to keep the car on the track in case it starts to spin around. The flaps will stay flat while the car is moving forward, but they're specially designed to flip up if the car goes into a spin, and will keep the car from becoming airborne. It's amazing how a feature that small could be so important!

On the inside, a stock car has a complex network of tubing that keeps the driver safe if his car flips onto its side or upside down, and roll bars form a protective cage designed to absorb the impact.

The Uniform – Casual To Customized

To the untrained eye, it may look like NASCAR drivers wear their uniforms just so they can be walking billboards for their sponsors. Not so. Underneath all those ads is a fire-retardant suit to keep the driver safe in case there's any combustion outside the engine. Special gloves and fire-resistant boots keep his hands and feet from burning up on the scalding steering wheel and hot metal gas pedal.

Even something as simple as a helmet is a safety factor. Each one is specially designed to fit a driver's head perfectly. If a driver gets into an accident, he'll have to have his helmet x-rayed to determine if there are any invisible cracks in it.

Some Restrictions Apply

All the modifications designed to protect a driver and his car won't help if there aren't any rules. The management of NASCAR has gone to great lengths to ensure that standards apply to every driver. And each car has to pass inspection before a race, to see that those standards are adhered to and to keep a level playing field.

The tragic deaths of Adam Petty, Kenny Irwin, Tony Roper and Dale Earnhardt (all within a one-year period) have caused many people to rethink NASCAR regulations.

There's certainly a question of safety when you're driving at speeds up to 200 mph. To slow things down a bit, two of NASCAR's super-speedways – Daytona and Talladega – have made restrictor plates mandatory, much to the chagrin of some drivers. A restrictor plate is designed to limit the air flow to the carbu-retor, reducing the car's speed. Many drivers and fans have protested the regulation, pointing out that these plates don't limit the speed by very much. Instead, they reduce speeds enough to bunch cars together on the track during a race. Cars

Dale Earnhardt pits at Daytona, where restrictor plates are required.

APWWP

AP/WWP

The HANS system protects a driver's head and neck from damage in a crash.

racing in such close proximity to each other can often mean more impact potential, leading to even greater hazards at the track. Many drivers believe that restrictor plates defeat the whole purpose of racing against each other, since they place a limit on speed.

Earnhardt's own tragic accident has prompted NASCAR officials to take a closer look at driver safety. A reasonably new device called a head and neck support (HANS) has recently been suggested as an additional precaution that might have prevented the deaths of Petty, Irwin, Roper and even Earnhardt. The HANS was designed to be strapped to a driver's seat belt and helmet, supporting his neck and preventing injuries. The device is already standard equipment for Formula One racing, although few NASCAR drivers use the HANS system at this time. Some believe that Dale Earnhardt wouldn't think of it, considering a HANS too restricting. The notion that such a device could have saved The Intimidator's life hasn't gone unchallenged. Nevertheless, since his accident, many drivers have been planning to start using the HANS device immediately.

HANS Off

Would the HANS device have saved Earnhardt? According to Dr. Steve Bohannon, "It's still a matter of speculation. Even if he had had the device on, [the crash] may have resulted in the same injuries."

To The Tracks And Back

Did you know that some of the innovations in your car come from recommendations made by NASCAR drivers? Although stock cars are specifically designed for superspeedways, sometimes their modifications also end up getting made to everyday-use cars, too.

What Next?

Sadly, accidents do happen. When cars speed along at more than 180 mph, it's almost inevitable. All the safety regulations in the world can't bring back NASCAR's cherished legends who lost their lives doing what they loved the most.

However, NASCAR has made outstanding strides to protect the lives of its drivers during the sport's history. The fans, friends and families of drivers lost to accidents hope that NASCAR will go on to learn from such tragedies in order to prevent them from happening again. It's hard to say just what the next safety innovations will be, but whatever they are, NASCAR will remain an invigorating sport, that's just that much safer for everyone on and off the track.

From the engine to the fuel tank, NASCAR continues to institute new safety features in efforts to prevent tragedies from occurring on the track.

Earnhardt
& The
History Of
NASCAR®

Legacy: How Earnhardt Transformed NASCAR®

More than any name or face, Dale Earnhardt represented NASCAR. Widely believed to be the greatest driver in stock car racing history, and certainly the sport's most popular member, Earnhardt was crucial in both expanding the sport's popularity and drawing in new fans. "Dale Earnhardt was the driver for NASCAR and played such an important role in all of our energy level and enthusiasm that has built NASCAR into what it is today," said organization president Mike Helton.

Along the way, Earnhardt developed an aggressive driving style that earned him the nickname The Intimidator. And he had an equally adept knack for marketing. He earned tens of millions of dollars for product sales and merchandise endorsements, which included everything from baseball caps to die-cast likenesses of his cars.

His career earnings, which totalled more than $41 million, were the highest in all of NASCAR, and the amount of money he accumulated through marketing deals was equally impressive.

Robert Laberge/Allsport

The Intimidator leads the pack at the Martinsville Speedway in 1999, followed by Mark Martin (Valvoline) and Mike Skinner (Lowe's).

NASCAR®'s Racy Roots

Stock car racing developed in the southeastern United States in the 1930s, at at time when a thriving moonshine industry supplied talented drivers adept at making quick runs.

Promotional Stunts

Early NASCAR drivers did what they could to draw attention to their sport. Tim Flock participated in 1952's races with a monkey – Jocko Flocko – in a crash helmet riding shotgun. Flock's brother Fonty had his own publicity stunt – he raced in shorts.

Before NASCAR's formation, several racing circuits peppered the region, each naming its own champion. The disorganization made the sport so difficult to cover that newspaper editors quit trying. But a meeting of promoters, mechanics and drivers in December of 1947 at Daytona Beach, Florida, changed all that.

With its 1948 inaugural season, NASCAR began to bring stock car racing under one set of rules with one champion each year. In its second season, NASCAR allowed only American stock cars – full-sized American cars – in its races. The first race, which took place in June 1949 in Charlotte, North Carolina, attracted thousands of fans and

AP/WWP

Lee Petty (#42) nosed ahead of Johnny Beauchamp (#73) for a win at the Daytona International Speedway on February 22, 1959.

Junior Johnson grins after winning the pole position at Atlanta on June 3, 1964.

AP/WWP

included stock family sedans. Jim Roper was the sport's first victor with his Lincoln.

Paved track events slowly gained popularity as the sport grew in popularity. Although its following was mostly southern, the races were no longer just in the South but in locations as far-reaching as New York and Wisconsin.

The sport developed a close relationship with car manufacturers, who provided a great deal of financial support. Their motto, "Win on Sunday, sell on Monday," reflected their belief that if their cars won the Sunday races, they would sell more easily in the showrooms. However, stock car racing lost five big stars during the 1960s through death and retirement. Soon, auto makers began to pull out their financial support.

That's when big tobacco's relationship with stock car racing developed. Racer Junior Johnson asked a friend who worked for tobacco-industry corporation R.J. Reynolds to sponsor his car for several hundred thousands of dollars. The timing was lucky for all parties involved, because the government had just banned cigarette advertising on television and R.J. Reynolds was looking for new ways to advertise. Out of this alliance grew the Winston Cup series, which Dale Earnhardt won seven times. It also brought a change in the number of NASCAR races.

7 & 7

Earnhardt and Richard Petty won the same number of Winston Cup championships. Earnhardt tied Petty's record by winning his seventh cup in 1994.

FAN CHECKERBEE GUIDE

AP/WWP

Richard "The King" Petty takes a break beside his #43, STP-sponsored car in 1981.

Earnhardt began his NASCAR career in 1975, just two years before the death of his father Ralph, who was the NASCAR Sportsman Champion in 1965.

Dale Earnhardt entered the circuit at a time when Richard Petty was king. Petty was the first person dominate the sport, and he holds the record for number of career wins. "Once you had an individual just dominating, it didn't make any difference if it was marble shooting, you know what I mean?" Petty told *Sports Illustrated*. "It was dominating a sport. When we were able to do what we did, we got recognition in New York, we got recognition in Canada, we got recognition in California."

In addition, Petty was charismatic and media-savvy. Besides encouraging media coverage and garnering national attention for the sport, he brought in fans. Over the years, Petty held many open houses and invited fans to stop by his front porch for an autograph.

From Petty, Earnhardt eventually inherited the mantle of being NASCAR's dominant personality – and then he ran away with it, taking the sport's popularity to new heights. Earnhardt came on strong to the racing scene. He was one of only four rookies at the time to have ever won a Grand National event and was the first to break $200,000 in winnings. He won rookie of the year honors in 1979. In 1980, Earnhardt won his first Winston Cup

Family Business

When asked how Earnhardt's family felt about him racing, he quipped, "Well, they started it." He explained, "Dad raced, so why can't I? My mom was pretty nervous about my dad, but she was really nervous about me. And [my wife's] father raced, so she's been in racing for a long time."

series championship, becoming the first NASCAR driver to win the Winston Cup a year after being named Rookie of the Year.

A Style To Intimidate

The biggest hero in NASCAR history was in many ways the perpetual anti-hero. From the beginning, Earnhardt's aggressive racing style made an impression on his competitors and fans. His rough driving and willingness to bump and cram any competitor who got in his way – sometimes causing him to spin and wreck off the track – earned him the nickname of The Intimidator.

In a dirt-track race in the 1970s, he bumped veteran driver Stick Elliott, causing Elliott's car to spin out. According to Earnhardt, after the race, somebody ran up to him to tell him that one of Elliott's mechanics was heading over with a pistol. "I ran out of the racetrack, jumped over the wall and took off," he told *Sports Illustrated*.

Buddy Baker, who won the Daytona 500 in 1980, told *The New York Times* that year that the young racer "doesn't know the meaning of pace" and "has more damn nerve than a sore tooth."

Although his fellow racers did not always appreciate Earnhardt's speed and tactics, the fans loved him for it and couldn't get enough of it. He added spice to the sport, gave spectators something to watch and, in the process, made NASCAR immensely popular, taking it from its southern roots to a nationwide following.

Dale Earnhardt was known for his sly grin and his black and white GM racing colors.

In February of 1985, just three laps from the finish at Richmond International Raceway, Earnhardt bumped Darrell Waltrip (older brother of 2001's Daytona winner, Michael Waltrip). Both cars spun into a wall and several cars behind them were destroyed in the process. NASCAR fined Earnhardt $5,000. They also put him on probation, but lifted it when he said that he had not meant to hit Waltrip's car.

In 1987, the legendary "pass in the grass" occurred. Earnhardt arrived at a Winston bonus race having already left a trail of very angry fellow racers behind him from the nine Winston cup races run so far that season. Other competitors resented him for running them off the track and engaging in tactics that many considered over-the-top. Even his own friend, Neil Bonnett, told *Sports Illustrated,* "If I can ever catch him, I'm gonna knock the s___ out of him."

Buddy Baker (#71) and Richard Petty (#43) battle for the 1973 Daytona win. AP/WWP

In the final 10-lap portion of the race, Earnhardt squeezed Bill Elliott into the apron, causing him to bump into Geoff Bodine. Bodine's car spun, Elliott's went high, and Earnhardt took the lead. After the caution, Earnhardt and Elliott traded traded paint at a turn. Squeezed in by Elliott, Earnhardt cut from the outside straight across his path. His left wheels ended up in the grass, but instead of spinning out of control, he managed to keep speed and bring his car back onto the track. Half a lap later, Earnhardt would jam Elliott toward the outside wall. Shortly thereafter, Elliott blew a tire and fell a lap behind, while Earnhardt went on to win. During the cool down lap, Elliott crashed his car into Earnhardt's as retribution. Bodine followed suit.

NASCAR fined Earnhardt for his behavior during the race and repri-manded the other Elliott and Bodine for their post-race antics. Officials may have disapproved of what occurred that day, but the fans ate it up.

Although famous for giving bumps on the track, Earnhardt was on the receiving end in 1996, when a bump from Sterling Marlin at Talladega sent him and his car airborne at 200 miles per hour. The vehicle's roof was crushed down to within six inches of the gear shift knob. Given the gravity of the wreck, Earnhardt got away with relatively minor injuries, which added to his mystique with fans. Not only was he a hard-driving, aggressive competitor, he was tough, able to take as good as he gave.

Earnhardt was "one tough customer" on the tracks, wearing Wrangler colors in 1986.

Although that accident left him unable to lift his left arm above his shoulder, he still managed to qualify for Indianapolis four days later. Two weeks after the crash, Earnhardt was lowered into his car for a qualifying run at Watkins Glen. He had to protect his ribs with a flak jacket and was fitted with a special harness to lift him out of the car in case there was a fire. Despite his pain and the fact that his left hand was immobilized, he managed to beat the track record by 0.3 of a second. And the racing legend continued to grow.

Even as he aged, his competitive spirit never faltered. Just two days before his death, he bumped a driver after an IROC race, sending that car into a spin, as retaliation for forcing

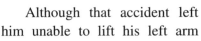

Intimidating

In 1988, Earnhardt nudged Geoff Bodine's car into the wall during the Coca-Cola 600 at Charlotte and the NASCAR penalty box was born. He was ordered to wait in the pits for several laps during the race as punishment. Although The Intimidator never quite behaved as extremely as he had after this event, his reputation was already sealed.

Earnhardt into the grass during the race. The Intimidator's own son, Dale Jr., has claimed to have been bumped by his father in a race. The fact that Earnhardt seemed to be blocking Sterling Marlin on the last lap of the Daytona 500 in order to preserve the win for Waltrip and a second-place finish for his son was even described as "uncharacteristic" by many in the media.

In a 1995 *Sports Illustrated* interview, Charlotte Motor Speedway president H.A. "Humpy" Wheeler (called "the savviest promoter in stock car racing"), attributed Earnhardt's popularity to what his driving style represented for fans. "I think everybody in the country is angry about having to drive in urban areas," said Wheeler. "They hate the traffic with a passion. Earnhardt drives through traffic too. And he won't put up with anything. He's going to get through. And that's what they want to do – but they can't. So Earnhardt is playing out their fantasies."

The fact that Earnhardt was no Richard Petty – who always was approachable and extremely available to all fans and media – did not matter when it came to popularity with the fans. "Earnhardt is the resurrected Confederate soldier," Wheeler said. "Where Petty was always compliant, Earnhardt will stand his ground and say, 'I'm not going to do that.' And the people who love him are the people who are told, every

AP/WWP

Intimidators don't cry, but they do accept defeat as Dale did when he was involved in a late-race crash in 1997's Daytona 500.

Over 20,000 fans looked on as Earnhardt cruised around Daytona's oval on Saturday, February 7, 1998.

day, what to do and what not to do, and they've got all those rules and regulations to go by. That just draws them closer to him."

And they were drawn in droves. At any Winston Cup race, one could find a sea of spectators donning Intimidator T-shirts and #3 hats, cars and vans with #3 emblazoned on them and motor homes painted in Earnhardt's black and silver colors.

Behind The Business Wheel

Earnhardt translated his popularity into big bucks. He was the Michael Jordan and Tiger Woods of NASCAR; not only did he excel at his sport, he soared in the marketing arena, blazing the commercial trail for other racers to follow.

Fittingly, his office complex in Mooresville, North Carolina, was known as the "garage-Mahal" and his 70-plus-foot yacht was named *Sunday Money*. To say that he transformed the marketing landscape of NASCAR may be an overstatement, given that he benefitted so far beyond what any other racer did. Perhaps it's more accurate to say he broadened the horizon, setting a standard of possibility no one would have previously imagined for a stock car racer.

Earnhardt made an appearance on a cable shopping network in 1993 and was a big hit – he sold almost $1 million worth of goods in two hours. In 1994, *Forbes* estimated he sold almost $50 million worth of souvenirs,

Earnhardt grabbed the checkered flag at the Winston 500 on October 15, 2000, in what would become his final victory. Kenny Wallace took second place and Joe Nemecheck pulled up in time to secure third.

pocketing about $5 million from the sales himself (some felt this number to be grossly undervalued).

In 1995, he bought Sports Image, Inc., the major distributor of his souvenirs, which marketed his image on everything from T-shirts to wall clocks. Earnhardt became the first and only driver to have complete control over his image, likeness, trademarks and copyrights. He also at least doubled his own cut of the take in the process. "When you own it, you have control over it and if it makes money, you make money," said Bill Battle, president of marketing firm Collegiate Concepts in a 1995 interview with *The Atlanta Journal and Constitution*. "But making money for Earnhardt is just a matter of how much . . . He's the Michael Jordan of stock car racing. He's head and shoulders above the next guy. He's a great driver with a mystique about him."

NASCAR And . . . Sneakers?

"Ten years ago people would have laughed if you said that a stock car driver from Kannapolis, North Carolina, would have a sneaker deal," said Don Hawk, vice president of Dale Earnhardt, Inc., in 1995. "I don't think anybody will be laughing in a year," he predicted.

Earnhardt's souvenirs were sold in trailer-sized rigs at the Winston Cup races, and in 1995, his agent said that his souvenir sales surpassed those of almost all the other drivers on the circuit combined. For fans, the price of living vicariously through Earnhardt varies. Anyone could have a memory of Earnhardt, from bumper stickers, socks and belt buckles to earrings, postcards and key chains, depending on what he or she wanted to spend.

After His Death

Ironically, one of Earnhardt's legacies could be a change in safety standards and rules for the sport that would keep racing at a level he would have surely disapproved of. He certainly liked to live and drive at full throttle and he complained after last year's Daytona 500 that the race bored him. Cars ran on the track in single-file with almost no passing. In an effort to encourage a more exciting race, NASCAR enacted aerodynamic rule changes this year, changes that Earnhardt had enthusiastically supported. The goal was to slow the cars and encourage closer, but unavoidably more dangerous, racing. They succeeded. The lead changed 49 times this year, 40 more than in the last race. Those who had been concerned about the safety of such a decision must have felt their worst

Bobby Labonte (#18) and Dale Earnhardt battle it out for first place in the Cracker Barrel 500 in March 2000 at Atlanta.

fears being confirmed. With 25 laps to go, nearly 20 cars were involved in one major accident (amazingly, no serious injuries resulted). And then of course, just before the finish, Earnhardt's car slammed into the wall one last time.

On the day after Earnhardt's death, several teams ordered a head and neck support (HANS) device that protects the driver's head neck from injuries. Earnhardt, who was one of the few drivers to still wear an open-faced helmet, did not wear a HANS device. Although some have speculated as to whether or not his life may have been saved with HANS, the doctor who treated him immediately after the accident said he doubted the device would have made a difference given the type of injuries Earnhardt sustained. It was later determined that a broken seat belt mechanism probably played a greater part in The Man In Black's injuries than the lack of the HANS device.

The life of Earnhardt may have ended on that track, but the legend will certainly live on, and most likely will continue to grow as a result.

20th Time's A Charm

Perhaps it's fitting that Earnhardt's final race was on a course where he had he failed to win its most famous race – The Daytona 500 – until his 20th try in 1998, marking one of the great moments in the sport.

After becoming airborne during a crash at Daytona in 1997, Earnhardt landed on top of Ernie Irvan's Havoline-sponsored car.

Earnhardt celebrated his 2000 Winston 500 win
under a shower of confetti.

The man who had seemed indestructible ended up dying in a crash that many deemed moderate – relatively speaking. Fans would swear they had seen him walk away from worse without a scratch, and they had expected him to do it again.

In his last race, Dale Earnhardt was not a winner, although racers from his team, including his own son, took first and second places. Earnhardt did go out setting a record of sorts. He is the only driver to date to be killed during the actual Daytona 500 competition.

Legendary Racers In Nascar® History

Since NASCAR was founded in 1948, hundreds of men and women have dreamed of a career racing the tracks in the NASCAR circuit. However, only a select few have had the determination to push the envelope no matter what the cost. Many have called Dale Earnhardt the greatest race car driver ever. Here's a look at some of the legendary legion of drivers who now seem larger than the sport itself.

Whether they've hailed from racing families or had a unique itch for speed, these drivers have broken records, made headlines and influenced the continual evolution of the sport that was born on the beaches of Daytona and is today a national phenomenon.

NOTE: Statistics listed through the end of the 2000 race season.

Bobby Allison

Hometown: Hueytown, AL
Birthdate: 12/3/37
Years Raced: 25
Starts: 718
Wins: 85
Pole Positions: 59
Retired: 1988

Buck Baker

Hometown: Charlotte, NC
Birthdate: 3/4/19
Years Raced: 26
Starts: 636
Wins: 46
Pole Positions: 44
Retired: 1976

Buddy Baker

Hometown: Charlotte, NC
Birthdate: 1/25/41
Years Raced: 34
Starts: 699
Wins: 19
Pole Positions: 40
Retired: 1994

Ralph Earnhardt

Hometown: Kannapolis, NC
Birthdate: 2/29/28
Years Raced: 6
Starts: 51
Wins: 0
Pole Positions: 1
Retired: 1964
Deceased: 9/26/73

Neil Bonnett

Hometown: Bessemer, AL
Birthdate: 7/30/46
Years Raced: 18
Starts: 363
Wins: 18
Pole Positions: 20
Deceased: 2/11/94

AP/WWP

Bill Elliott

Hometown: Dawsonville, GA
Birthdate: 10/8/55
Years Raced: 26
Starts: 591
Wins: 40
Pole Positions: 49
Active Driver

AP/WWP

Tim Flock

Hometown: Ft. Payne, AL
Birthdate: 5/11/24
Years Raced: 13
Starts: 187
Wins: 39
Pole Positions: 39
Retired: 1961

© DAYTONA RACING ARCHIVES

Ned Jarrett

Hometown: Newton, NC
Birthdate: 10/12/32
Years Raced: 13
Starts: 352
Wins: 50
Pole Positions: 35
Retired: 1966

AP/WWP

A.J. Foyt

Hometown: Houston, TX
Birthdate: 1/16/35
Years Raced: 31
Starts: 128
Wins: 7
Pole Positions: 10
Retired: 1994

© DAYTONA RACING ARCHIVES

Junior Johnson

Hometown: Ronda, NC
Birthdate: 6/28/31
Years Raced: 14
Starts: 313
Wins: 50
Pole Positions: 47
Retired: 1966

Alan Kulwicki

Hometown: Greenfield, WI
Birthdate: 12/14/54
Years Raced: 9
Starts: 207
Wins: 5
Pole Positions: 24
Deceased: 4/1/93

David Pearson

Hometown: Spartanburg, SC
Birthdate: 12/22/34
Years Raced: 27
Starts: 574
Wins: 105
Pole Positions: 113
Retired: 1986

Benny Parsons

Hometown: Detroit, MI
Birthdate: 7/12/41
Years Raced: 21
Starts: 526
Wins: 21
Pole Positions: 20
Retired: 1988

Lee Petty

Hometown: Level Cross, NC
Birthdate: 3/14/14
Years Raced: 16
Starts: 427
Wins: 54
Pole Positions: 18
Retired: 1964
Deceased: 4/5/00

Richard Petty

Hometown: Level Cross, NC
Birthdate: 7/2/37
Years Raced: 35
Starts: 1184
Wins: 200
Pole Positions: 126
Retired: 1992

Ricky Rudd

Hometown: Chesapeake, VA
Birthdate: 9/12/56
Years Raced: 27
Starts: 628
Wins: 19
Pole Positions: 25
Active Driver

Fireball Roberts

Hometown: Daytona Beach, FL
Birthdate: 1/20/29
Years Raced: 15
Starts: 206
Wins: 33
Pole Positions: 35
Deceased: 7/2/64

Darrell Waltrip

Hometown: Franklin, TN
Birthdate: 2/5/47
Years Raced: 30
Starts: 749
Wins: 84
Pole Positions: 59
Retired: 2000

Joe Weatherly
Hometown: Norfolk, VA
Birthdate: 5/29/22
Years Raced: 12
Starts: 230
Wins: 25
Pole Positions: 19
Deceased: 1/19/64

Cale Yarborough
Hometown: Timmonsville, SC
Birthdate: 3/27/39
Years Raced: 31
Starts: 559
Wins: 83
Pole Positions: 70
Retired: 1988

Dale Earnhardt
Hometown: Kannapolis, NC
Birthdate: 4/29/51
Years Raced: 26
Starts: 675
Wins: 76
Pole Positions: 22
Deceased: 2/18/01

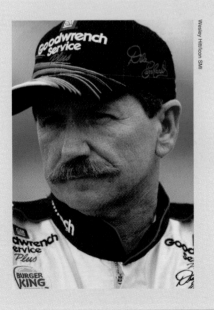

Wesley Hitt/Icon SMI

Racing At Daytona

With its sandy beaches and pristine waters, the shoreline of Florida's Daytona Beach seems to be an unlikely spot for the supercharged, gas-guzzling excitement of stock car racing. Yet, it is this very spot where NASCAR was born. Years before Daytona International Speedway, the "World Center of Racing," was built, races were held along Daytona's flat beaches. Drivers didn't race near the beach – they raced *on* it – and its flat, hard sand was perfect for drivers looking for speed and spills!

On The Beach

Stock car racing was common on Daytona Beach since the 1930s, but it took the giant vision of one man to transform the world of stock car racing into a legitimate sports phenomenon.

Salt Water In The Radiator!

During the early days of racing at the Daytona Beach-Road course, drivers took a thrilling ride through the spraying surf and over sandy turf. Races sometimes had to be cancelled when the tide came in!

Welcome to Daytona! Daytona Beach is home to racing's most famous track.

William H. G. France settled his family in Daytona Beach in 1934. France, a mechanic and auto enthusiast, became a common sight on the Daytona Beach stock car scene. He was soon promoting stock car events and, by the 1940s, was looking for something bigger to bring to Daytona. Meeting at the Streamline Hotel on Daytona Beach from December 14-17, 1947, France and his associates formulated a firm set of guidelines, enforcement powers and point systems for stock car racing. They named their organization the National Association of Stock Car Auto Racing (NASCAR) – and the story began.

From The Sand . . .

With "Big Bill" as its president, NASCAR wasted little time in establishing itself as stock car racing's premier association. Daytona hosted the first NASCAR race, a Modified race held along the beach and before 1948 came to a close, over 50 NASCAR races had taken place – all before the creation of the Daytona International Speedway.

While this sandy terrain was popular among drivers and fans, the future of beach racing looked uncertain. An increase in beachfront developments squeezed the racers from their sandy home, so predicting that beach races would soon become a thing of the past, Big Bill began his big plan for Daytona.

. . . To The Superspeedway

France envisioned a race track that could serve as a showplace for the excitement of NASCAR. With that idea in mind, work began on the

In addition to hosting the Daytona 500, Daytona International Speedway is also the site of the Pepsi 400.

Daytona International Speedway in the mid-1950s. This track was radically different than the road courses it replaced. Here, drivers had the opportunity to reach nearly unheard-of speeds on the fast-racing, 2.5-mile track with high-banked turns.

The first race at the Daytona International Speedway was the Daytona 500 on the 22nd day of February, 1959 – just over 42 years ago. The legendary Lee Petty won the inaugural event in the closest race in Daytona's history. In fact, driver Johnny Beauchamp had been declared the winner but, after three days, the race officials reviewed photos of the two drivers crossing the finish line and then reversed their decision.

Racing patriarch Lee Petty won the first Daytona 500 in 1959.

The Daytona 500 soon began to be acknowledged as the "Super Bowl" of stock car racing and since has had several notable finishes in its storied career. For the first time ever, scenes from the 1979 Daytona 500 were televised across America and even featured Bobby Allison in a fistfight with Cale Yarborough after Cale had sent Bobby's brother Donnie into the wall. Incidentally, that Daytona 500 was also won by a Petty – Lee's son, Richard, whose seven Winston Cup championships tie him with only one man – Dale Earnhardt.

Like Father, Like Son

Just as Richard had followed in his father's footsteps, so too did Dale Earnhardt. The son of stock car racer Ralph Earnhardt, the younger

Richard Petty grins ear-to-ear after winning his third Daytona 500 in 1971.

Earnhardt discovered at an early age that auto racing was in his blood.

Earnhardt's first ride was a pink 1956 Ford Victoria, but it was not until 1975 that he made his debut on the Winston Cup circuit. But driving a blue and yellow Dodge Charger, Earnhardt saw limited action.

It wasn't until 1979 that Earnhardt began his rookie season in earnest and was seen as a serious threat. But while Earnhardt made history as the first driver to claim Rookie of the Year honors as well as the Winston Cup championship in the same year, victory at the Daytona 500 was still nearly 20 years away.

Close But No Cigar

Even before the tragic events of February 18, 2001, Dale Earnhardt and the track at Daytona had been in conflict. For years, the Daytona 500 race had been a fierce dragon, constantly taunting and teasing Earnhardt with its fire-breathing, 2.5-mile tri-oval track.

All the while, Earnhardt, The Intimidator every step of the way, refused to be beaten by the track.

And those 20 years contained several oh-so-close finishes, the first occurring in 1986. That was the year Earnhardt battled Geoff Bodine and had a legitimate shot at taking the checkered flag, until Earnhardt was forced to pit after running out of gas.

The Small Screen Brings The Oval Track Into Your Living Room

The 1979 Daytona 500 was the first NASCAR race televised in its entirety – all five hours of it!

In 1990, Earnhardt came close again, only to

have victory snatched away when a flat tire took him out of the running and paved the way for Derrike Cope to speed by and take the flag. Earnhardt's Daytona drought was again prolonged by Dale Jarrett, who bested him in both 1993 and 1996, each race decided by mere tenths of a second. Then in the 1997 Daytona 500, Earnhardt ended up upside down after trading paint with Jeff Gordon and Dale Jarrett. Earnhardt was ushered into an ambulance but, in true "Intimidator" fashion, jumped out of the ambulance when he saw that his smashed car still had its tires intact.

Fans knew that Earnhardt intended to finish every race as long as he had a car to carry him. He would have walked to the finish line if necessary!

Victory – At Last!

By all accounts, the 1998 Daytona 500 was a memorable experience for everyone involved. It was there, on racing's most famous course, at racing's most famous event, that Earnhardt won the event that had eluded him for so long.

Speedweeks

The fun starts early at The Daytona 500! Two weeks before race day, the festivities begin with several auto events including the star-studded Bud Shootout, Busch Series racing and Craftsman Truck Series races.

AP/WWP

Dale Earnhardt (#2) challenges Neil Bonnett (#21) as the checkered flag waves during the Firecracker 400 at Daytona International Speedway.

But what a win it was! Earnhardt had been having a disappointing run of luck with no wins on the Winston Cup circuit in almost two years. But this time, he found the right combination of a "good crew, a strong engine, a well-handling car and the man who was going to win – and have luck on his side, too."

With two laps remaining, Earnhardt was leading but was being followed closely by Jeremy Mayfield and Bobby Labonte. On the backstretch, however, a couple of cars got tangled up and the caution flag went up, instructing the drivers to hold their position. But the white flag also went up – indicating that there was only one lap remaining in the race. The only thing that Earnhardt had to do was drive home and not trip over his shoelaces! Victory was at hand . . . and it was sweet!

By finally slaying the dragon at Daytona, Earnhardt also silenced the naysayers who had doubted his ability to win the big race.

Dale's Destiny

Former driver Jimmy Johnson explains the mystique of Daytona: "Some tracks separate the men from the boys. This track will separate the brave from the weak when the boys are gone." Dale Earnhardt may be gone, but his bravery at Daytona will be forever remembered by racing fans all over the world.

Dale Earnhardt celebrates victory after winning his first Daytona 500 on February 15, 1998.

Track Guide

In his more than 20 years on the NASCAR circuit, Dale Earnhardt raced on all kinds of Winston Cup circuit tracks, new and old. For 2001, there were 23 operating Winston Cup tracks, including two road courses, one rectangular track and a variety of oval tracks, all offering both fans and drivers a unique racing experience. No matter what the track design, The Man In Black left his mark.

Atlanta Motor Speedway
Hampton, Georgia

The Atlanta Motor Speedway hosts two Winston Cup races each year. Atlanta also hosts an annual Busch series race, music festivals and other civic events.

FACT: Dale Earnhardt won his 75th Winston Cup race at Atlanta on March 12, 2000, at the Cracker Barrel 500.

Bristol Motor Speedway
Bristol, Tennessee

Known as "The World's Fastest Half Mile," the track at Bristol hosts two Winston races per season, including one of the Winston Cup's only night events. The half-mile track has 36-degree banking, the steepest of all NASCAR tracks.

FACT: Dale Earnhardt had his first Winston Cup victory at Bristol in April 1979 at the Southeastern 500.

California Speedway
Fontana, California

The California Speedway is one of NASCAR's newest tracks. In its years of operation, the smooth two-mile, tri-oval has gained a reputation as being a favorite among drivers.

FACT: Dale Earnhardt was involved in a five-car accident at this track during the 1998 California 500. The Intimidator still finished ninth, a great feat considering he entered the race on a past champions provisional.

Chicagoland Speedway
Joliet, Illinois

One of two new tracks to be added to the NASCAR circuit in 2001, Chicagoland Speedway will host its first Winston Cup race on July 15, 2001. This 1.5-mile track is a D-shaped oval that features 11-degree banking on the front stretch and 5-degree banking on the back stretch.

FACT: Chicagoland will be one of the first tracks to bring NASCAR to the Midwest.

Darlington Raceway
Darlington, South Carolina

Drivers have been racing at Darlington since 1950. Considered the "Toughest Track to Tame" because of its egg-like shape and varied turn degrees, it's hard for drivers to leave the 1.3-mile track without a "Darlington Stripe" on their cars, the traditional sign of inadvertent wall contact.

FACT: On March 3, 1993, Dale Earnhardt set the Darlington speed record of 139.958 mph during the TransSouth Financial 500.

Daytona International Speedway
Daytona Beach, Florida

Home to numerous motorsports events through-out the year, Daytona International is NASCAR's most famous track. The 2.5-mile tri-oval hosts the Daytona 500, the Winston Cup's most renowned race.

FACT: On his 20th attempt at the Daytona 500 on February 15, 1998, Dale Earnhardt finally claimed his first Daytona 500 victory.

Dover Downs
International Speedway
Dover, Delaware

The "Monster Mile" is a cement oval with a lap of exactly one mile. Considered one of the most exciting tracks at which to watch a race north of the Carolinas, Dover Downs has run two Winston Cup races annually since 1971.

FACT: Dale Earnhardt won both races at Dover in 1989. Mark Martin took second and Ken Schrader came in third at both races.

Homestead-Miami Speedway
Miami, Florida

The inaugural Winston Cup Series race at this 1.5-mile Florida track was held in November 1999. Prior to 1999, the Homestead-Miami Speedway was used primarily for the Craftsman Truck and Busch circuit races.

FACT: At his first race on the Miami track, Dale Earnhardt pulled up from the 23rd starting position to finish in the top 10.

Indianapolis Motor Speedway
Speedway, Indiana

Nicknamed "The Brickyard" because the track was originally brick-paved, Indianapolis became part of the Winston Cup circuit in 1994. Known best as the home of Indy car racing, Indianapolis's 2.5-mile rectangular track is home to the Brickyard 400.

FACT: Dale Earnhardt set the Brickyard's Winston Cup speed record (155.206 mph) on August 5, 1995.

Kansas Speedway
Kansas City, Kansas

In 2001, Kansas Speedway's inaugural season, the tri-oval track set industry records for first-season ticket sales. This is due in part to the track's fan-friendly atmosphere, which provides spectacular views from every seat in the arena.

FACT: Kansas Speedway is expected to be the largest tourist attraction in the state of Kansas.

Las Vegas Motor Speedway
Las Vegas, Nevada

This tri-oval, 1.5-mile track located in the "Entertainment Capital Of The World" provides drivers with plenty of passing room, making for an enthralling race every year.

FACT: With his eighth-place finish in the 1998 Las Vegas 400, Dale Earnhardt had the only Chevrolet to finish in the top 10 at Las Vegas' inaugural race.

Lowe's Motor Speedway
Concord, North Carolina

This North Carolina track hosts The Winston Select, NASCAR's all-star race held each May. Like the California Speedway, Lowe's is a favorite among drivers with its roomy 1.5-mile tri-oval track.

FACT: Dale Earnhardt's first Winston Cup career start was at Lowe's, then called Charlotte Motor Speedway, at the World 600 in 1975.

Martinsville Speedway
Martinsville, Virginia

The smallest (0.526 miles) and oldest (1955) track on the NASCAR race schedule, Martinsville was originally a dirt track and remains the perfect place to trade paint on a Sunday afternoon.

FACT: Dale Earnhardt won his first Martinsville race in September 1980, driving Rod Osterlund's #2 Chevrolet in the Old Dominion 500.

Michigan Speedway
Brooklyn, Michigan

Located near Detroit, the 2-mile Michigan Speedway has one of the widest laps in NASCAR racing. It's no surprise to sometimes see three and four cars racing abreast on the D-shaped oval.

FACT: Michigan Speedway's closest finish was recorded at the 1998 IROC race when Dale Earnhardt and Dale Earnhardt Jr. raced for the checkered flag.

New Hampshire International Speedway
Loudon, New Hampshire

Loudon, the only NASCAR racetrack in New England, hosts two Winston Cup races annually. The 1.5-mile track is similar to Martinsville and offers extreme racing through 12-degree turns and 5-degree straightaways.

FACT: In 1999, Dale Earnhardt qualified for pole position time just fractions of a second behind his son Dale Jr. for the Jiffy Lube 300.

North Carolina Speedway
Rockingham, North Carolina

Otherwise known as "The Rock," this one-mile oval racetrack in North Carolina has traditionally hosted the second race of the Winston Cup season and is known for its rough surface, which inflates tire damage.

FACT: In 1993, Dale Earnhardt took second place to Rusty Wallace at Rockingham in both the GM Goodwrench 500 in February and the AC Delco 500 in October.

Phoenix International Raceway
Phoenix, Arizona

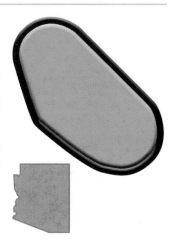

This D-shaped, one-mile desert track is known for its complex turns and majestic surroundings. Since 1964, the raceway has been host to all divisions of racing.

FACT: Dale Earnhardt has had five top-five finishes at Phoenix since it hosted its first Winston Cup Series race in 1988.

Pocono Raceway
Long Pond, Pennsylvania

Pocono Raceway is a superspeedway and road course all in one package. When preparing for a race at Pocono, drivers must build their cars to conquer tight turns and thrilling straightaways on the 2.5-mile triangle.

FACT: Dale Earnhardt won his first race at Pocono in the Summer 500 on July 19, 1987.

Richmond International Raceway
Richmond, Virginia

Racers and fans have frequented Richmond since its dirt-track days in the 1940s. Redesigned to accommodate today's stock cars, the three-quarter-mile track is an enjoyable site for fans and drivers alike.

FACT: Dale Earnhardt swept the 1987 Richmond series, taking first place in both the Miller High Life 500 and the Wrangler Jeans Indigo 400.

Sears Point Raceway
Sonoma, California

Sears Point, one of two road courses on the Winston Cup circuit, is marked by hills and valleys unique to the Sonoma Valley. The 11-turn course is almost two miles long and hosts one race annually.

FACT: Dale Earnhardt has recorded four top-five finishes since the track's first Winston Cup race in June 1989.

Talladega Superspeedway
Talladega, Alabama

Talladega is considered to be the fastest race-track on the NASCAR circuit. Racers have set world speed records on this Alabama racetrack that stretches just more than 2.5 miles in length.

FACT: Dale Earnhardt won what would become his final race at this racetrack on October 15, 2000.

Texas Motor Speedway
Fort Worth, Texas

The second-largest sports arena in the country, this quad-oval speedway runs 1.5 miles with 24-degree banking in the turns. With its resort-like amenities, fans flock to Fort Worth Speedway every year.

FACT: Dale Earnhardt has finished on average in approximately 16th place at his races at Texas Motor Speedway.

Watkins Glen International
Watkins Glen, New York

Known for its unusual right-hand turns, this upstate New York track has been host to many road-racing series. NASCAR held its first race here in 1957.

FACT: On August 9, 1996, Dale Earnhardt set the top qualifying time on the 2.45-mile road course with a speed of 120.733 mph.

The Race Day Experience

Watching a race on television just doesn't compare to the experience of being trackside on race weekend. But if you're a NASCAR newcomer, there are a few things you should know before you head off to watch the action live.

Getting There Is Half The Fun

It's not a bad idea to start planning a trek out to the tracks a year ahead of time. Major races like the Daytona 500 often sell out months in advance. Tickets, which range in price from reasonable to in the triple-digits, can be hard to obtain last-minute, but it's certainly not impossible, depending on the race and the venue. Tickets can be purchased through track box offices or on the Internet, if the track has a web site.

Vantage Point

Most fans sit in the grandstands, but some tracks allow for seating in the infield – the circular green on the inside of the track. Fans usually drive their cars or motor homes onto the infield and set up camp on top

The crowd – a sell out – watches as the
Daytona 500 gets under way.

Can't make it to the race track? These fans head to the local pool hall in the heart of Bill Elliott country to cheer on their favorite driver.

of them to get a view of the track. It can be pretty hard to see all of the action from the middle, but when the grandstands are sold out, the infield is usually still available. It may be crowded, but it's the perfect spot to get to know other fans and cheer for your favorite drivers in the absolute center of the action. There's nothing like participating in a virtual block party with 43 cars screaming around the track just a few feet away!

Nothing compares to being there

What Do Those Flags Mean?

- Green – Signals the beginning of the race or the restart of the race after any cautions.

- Yellow – Tells drivers to maintain their positions due to dangerous conditions on the track.

- Red – Temporarily stops the race after crashes for a thorough track clean-up.

- Black – Tells a driver that he has either broken a rule or his car is a hazard to those around him and he has to pit.

- Black with White Cross – Signals that a driver's laps are no longer being counted. Second warning after black flag.

- Blue with Orange Stripe – Tells drivers who are a lap down to yield to the lead cars.

- White – Signals the beginning of the last lap.

- Checkered – Means the race is over.

– the distinctive smell of burning rubber and the roar of stock cars running full-throttle three and four wide on NASCAR's most famous tracks. Anticipation hangs in the air at any race, and not only about the day's winner. What will Jeff Gordon's new paint scheme look like? Will Tony Stewart land in the top five? Will Dale Jr. place above Matt Kenseth? Even if you only follow one driver, you can't help but get caught up in the excitement around you – especially if you're sitting next to fans of a different driver!

NASCAR fans know that sitting in the grandstands is an intense experience. Stock car racing is touted as a family sport, so it's likely that you'll be surrounded by adults and kids of all ages, and they may all be cheering for different drivers! Just remember that it's all in good fun and that fans can sometimes be a rowdy bunch, especially if their driver isn't doing so well.

It's The Pits

Whether it's a scheduled stop or an emergency situation, watching pit stops is almost more fun than watching the race itself. And if you have a stopwatch handy, you can time the fellas in front of and behind the wall to see if they're losing time or breaking records!

Race fans will tell you that nothing beats being able to watch the race from the infield!

The action at the races isn't just limited to the track – the pit is exciting, too!

APWWP

Pit crews are essential to the success of a driver. Drivers handpick their crews and trust them to install tires correctly, diagnose (and repair!) engine problems on the spot, and fill up the gas tank – all at the same time! They work like a well-greased engine, and watching them work is an incredible adrenaline rush.

For some drivers, the turn onto pit road may be the last turn of the race, especially if they know that there's a problem with their car. Pit crews may be experts, but sometimes it's just not safe to return to the track for more laps at a grueling 200 mph.

"Looks Like He's Outta The Race, Folks"

What happens if your driver's engine fails or if he gets disqualified during the race? You could hang around and watch the rest of the action, or you can walk around the miles of souvenir stands and team haulers in the parking lots. From shirts and hats to die-cast cars and radio

What To Bring

Make sure you go to the track prepared for any situation. Here's a quick checklist:

- Binoculars
- Sunscreen
- Radio with earphones
- Raincoat/umbrella
- Earplugs
- Camera with high-powered lens
- A fine-tip permanent marker and one or two items to be signed, just in case you run into your favorite driver in the garage.
- Apparel with your driver's logo on it

The Race Day Experience

FAN CHECKERBEE GUIDE

119

scanners (to tune into specific drivers' radio frequencies), dealers and retailers are out there selling everything imaginable with your favorite driver's likeness, number or signature on it.

And because many times drivers are easily accessible to the fans after the race, there's a good chance that you might run into your favorite NASCAR hero and he might even sign one of your new souvenirs! Walking around the grounds may also yield plenty of outstanding photo opportunities of drivers and cars that will help you remember your special day at the tracks.

Of course, when the hot sun gets the better of you and you're looking for a little quiet, some tracks have recreation areas, like lakes or ponds (or beaches, like at Daytona) that can be quite relaxing after you've gone hoarse from cheering. And if it's shade you're looking for, try to stop by the garage to catch some behind-the-scenes action.

Weather Or Not

Most race tracks are located in the southern states where racing season lasts for the majority of the year. NASCAR races are notorious for stopping and starting unexpectedly due to brief spurts of inclement weather. So, prepare to be rained on now and again! But never fear, there's plenty to see and do around the track while you're waiting for the rain delay to end and the track to dry out.

Fans trudge through the rain showers as the crew members for driver Scott Pruett work on his Tide Ford in the garage.

Inside Track

Being in the garage is an experience! While the press tends to hover around the drivers, so do the fans – and drivers are usually more than willing to sign autographs and share a few words with their devoted followers. Did you think that Dale Jr. made an exceptionally exciting move on the straightaway dur-

These fans enjoy the action high above the Phoenix International Raceway.

ing lap 87? Well, this is your chance to tell him! And if he had a bad day at the track, let him know that his fans still support him.

Of course, drivers spend a lot of time in the garage before the race perfecting their cars and much time after the race figuring out what went wrong, so be courteous to those working around you and watch where you're going – no one wants to run over a fan!

Since the NASCAR garage is where all the off-track action is, the average fan may not be able to get a garage pass with much ease, but they are out there, if you know the right people. Some tracks even sell them like they sell tickets, so ask around.

Whether you're sipping lemonade atop a motor home in the infield, adding to the stomping, clamoring and chanting in the grandstands or checking out the off-track action and excitement, there's no bad place to be on race day.

Dale, The Businessman

The Business Of Being Earnhardt

The pilgrimage started early Sunday evening, just after the announcement was made that NASCAR had lost its hero and friend, Dale Earnhardt. Where could you go to make a memorial, to leave a note or to just say a prayer?

Many of Earnhardt's fans found themselves heading to the tiny southern town of Mooresville, North Carolina, the town that Earnhardt called home. Known as "Race City, USA," Mooresville was home base to The Intimidator and many of the other "movers and shakers" in the racing community. It is home to more stock car teams than anywhere else in the country – it is where they come to build, fix, tune, paint and decal their cars every week in one of the many race shops located in town. This is the town that Earnhardt built.

Going Home

Earnhardt was born in Kannapolis – less than 10 minutes away from Mooresville – and has always stayed close to his family and to the community that embraced its hometown hero with friendship and pride.

Up the road a piece, in Mooresville, is the "Garage Mahal," the glitzy multi-million–dollar race shop/showroom/gift store/museum that houses Earnhardt's business offices, Dale Earnhardt Incorporated (DEI). Although the gates were

AP/WWP

Mourners came to Dale Earnhardt Inc. to leave gifts and grieve for Dale.

closed, this is where fans came to say goodbye. They left momentos, flowers, handwritten notes and tears.

The flags flew at half-mast over the corporate headquarters that were ruled by Earnhardt – the entrepreneur and the icon, but also the husband, son and father. How did he do it? How did this kid who never graduated from high school become the business tycoon who landed several times on the *Forbes* magazine list of top celebrity money-maker athletes?

Just A Boy With Big Toys

Earnhardt became one of the most successful in the field of racing – and in the field of life. He owned three racing teams and managed to garner millions of dollars in earnings through licensing and souvenir agreements, endorsement deals and a Chevrolet dealership. Additionally, Earnhardt profited through leasing out the seats he purchased on the New York and American Stock Exchanges.

Dale signed driver Michael Waltrip to his team in 2000.

He also owned a 400-acre farm in Mooresville – the property that boasts the offices and staff of DEI. On his farm, he enjoyed the trappings of country life by raising chicken and cattle and fishing in the nearby pond that he stocked with catfish and bream. To keep up with his schedule of personal appearances, business and racing commitments, Earnhardt had his own private Learjet.

The Merchandise Machine

Around the time that Earnhardt married Teresa in 1982, he was thinking about the future of his career and made some decisions that would enable him to achieve his elite status in the racing community and the unbelievable wealth that he realized within 20 years.

Understanding the potential value of his name, one of the things that Earnhardt did was trademark that and his image early in his career – one of the first race drivers to do so. In another sound business move, Earnhardt hired Don Hawk in 1993 to oversee the marketing of his image. Within a few years, fans could find The Man In Black on everything from billiard cues to fishing lures.

Endorsements of products provided Earnhardt with the means to build his empire. According to *Forbes* magazine, his income topped $15.5 million in 1997, only to increase to $24 million in 1998 and $26.5 million in 1999. When Earnhardt was asked about his earnings and how he was handling that aspect of his success, he replied, "I don't know. Teresa has it all. I sign autographs and drive race cars." And he enjoyed every minute of it.

Action . . . In The Wings

Action Performance, the premier motorsports collectibles distributor, and Earnhardt have had a lengthy relationship ever since Action first bought rights from him in the mid-1990s to distribute a line of die-cast collectibles featuring the #3 "GM Goodwrench" and #3 "Wrangler" cars. In fact, Earnhardt was the first license that the racing promotion and distribution company ever made. Fred Wagenhals, the founder and CEO of this Arizona-based company says, "[my wife and I] sold our house, took the last $300,000 we had to our name, and gave it to Dale for his license. I knew that he was the guy that I could build the cornerstone of my business around."

By 1996, Earnhardt was one of the company's

---

1 . . . 2 . . .

When Earnhardt was invited to address the National Press Club luncheon in 1998, Club president Doug Harbrecht introduced the racer as "a god in this business," and went on to say that "In North Carolina, the way they count is one, two, Dale Earnhardt, four, five, six."

---

official spokesmen and Wagenhals had purchased Earnhardt's company, Sports Image Inc., which marketed and distributed his racing related souvenirs, T-shirts and memorabilia. By 1998, Earnhardt was endorsing Action's Performance Plus Nutritional products, a line of power bars and vitamins – marketed for individuals who "strive for the 'racer's edge.'"

Sponsoring #3

NASCAR drivers couldn't achieve the technological advances that keep them competitive if not for the financial backing provided by corporate sponsors. Fans identify racers by their cars, which are often called "moving billboards," with their distinctive colors and company logos incorporated into the car's design.

GM Goodwrench Service Plus, the parts and service division of General Motors, has been Earnhardt's primary sponsor since 1988 when Wrangler bowed out.

Coca-Cola, a recognized household brand name for years, has been

These die-cast collectibles show off just some of The Intimidator's many paint schemes.

the official soft drink of NASCAR since 1997 and one of Earnhardt's associate sponsors since 1998. That turned out to be a profitable decision for the soft drink company, as 1998 was also the year that Earnhardt won the Daytona 500 – and celebrated in Victory Lane with a bottle of Coke clutched in his raised hand.

Other associate sponsors for Earnhardt's team include AC Delco, Burger King and Snap-On Tools, whose company logos are featured near the windows, as well as on the rear panels and sides of Earnhardt's car.

Batter Up!

Late last year, the announcement came that the Piedmont Boll Weevils – a minor league baseball team from Kannapolis – was changing its name to the Kannapolis Intimidators. No doubt, the name would be more intimidating to the opposing teams, but the main reason for the change was the change in team ownership. Yes, Kannapolis native Dale Earnhardt had bought a portion of the team.

Dale celebrates his long-awaited victory at the 1998 Daytona 500.

The new name made it necessary to come up with a new team logo, which was provided by NASCAR's premier artist and illustrator, Sam Bass. Bass is responsible for Earnhardt's image on the Wheaties cereal box and he designs the cars for Earnhardt's team and for Hendrick Motorsports. Bass was more than happy to design the logo for Earnhardt's newest venture. The result was an imposing personification of the letter "K," complete with a scowl, fangs and a clawed hand clutching a baseball. Now, *that's* called intimidation!

Wheelin' & Dealin'

Earnhardt's interest in cars carried over into his ownership of an automobile dealership in nearby Newton, North Carolina. Dale Earnhardt Chevrolet has proven to be a mecca for Earnhardt's fans. He often stopped in to sign autographs and meet the public. And his fondness for the Chevrolet name has been evident throughout his driving career.

For the past 16 years, Earnhardt drove a Chevy Monte Carlo or a Chevy Lumina, which resulted in over 60 of his total career wins. But what he loved most was driving the older model Chevy cars. "(During the 1980s), we raced cars that were basically bullet-proof," he said. "We'd scuff the wall with them or get into a bump-up, and you could still race and win."

Owning The Boys

For many of Earnhardt's fans, watching him throughout his career of almost 30 years has been a study in Success 101. As a driver, Earnhardt excelled, and with that experience, he was turning to another aspect of racing – that of team ownership for Dale Earnhardt Jr., Steve Park and Michael Waltrip as part of the DEI business. Because of Earnhardt's financial resources, he was able to provide funding for the best in equipment and personnel for his teams. Steve Park commented on Earnhardt's generosity and commitment to his drivers this way: "Man, Dale Earnhardt has just built us an awesome shop and given us the tools we need to compete. It will attract the type of people we want on this Pennzoil team. This sport is difficult enough without having to worry about the equipment and the workplace, and we sure don't have any of those kinds of worries."

Taking lessons from his team owner Richard Childress Earnhardt invested his time and money into building a team of new, young and promising race car drivers. Some saw this change as an indication of his future retirement from driving, but others just could not accept that possibility. In an interview in 1998, Earnhardt hinted as his future as team owner with the words, "I turn 50 in three years, and I don't know whether I want to race past that or not." Then, again, in a January 2001 interview, Earnhardt emphatically stated, "I've never considered retirement. Ain't even thought about it. Hell, I'm just startin' to reach my peak!"

Dale Earnhardt Jr.

In June 1998, Dale Earnhardt Jr. – also known as "Little E" – and his dad formally entered into an agreement in which the son, under a 5-year contract with an option for an additional 5 years, would drive for DEI. The elder Earnhardt was pleased with the deal but stressed that the close relationship with his son was always paramount, saying that "It feels good to finally have a formal contract signed with Earnhardt Jr., but our blood contract has been good for 23 years

Proving His Worth

Before Dale Jr. and his dad signed a 5-year deal in 1998, young Dale only had a "handshake" agreement to drive for his dad. $500 plus a percentage of race winnings was Dale Jr.'s weekly salary.

and that will always be the most important contract I have with him."

It is true that Earnhardt Jr. was only 23 years old when he signed on with his dad, but the younger Earnhardt had already consistently ranked in the top five in Grand National point standings and had driven to win twice in the series that season before signing with his father (he went on to Victory Lane 5 more times that year, for a total of 7 wins in 1998.) In addition, Earnhardt Jr. was considered one of the hottest properties in both talent and marketing potential in 1998.

Dale Jr. joined his father on the Winston Cup circuit.

Today, Earnhardt Jr. is becoming one of the most popular drivers on the NASCAR circuit. He has embraced his fans by making himself accessible to the public – he has an official web site (*www.dalejr.com*) and is a regular guest on live chats on the Internet. And he recently appeared in *PEOPLE* magazine as one of the "Sexy Men of 2000."

Steve Park

Steve Park had a dream. "When I was racing modifieds I set a goal of either being in or on my way to Winston Cup racing by the time I was 30," he explains. At 23, with no money and no major sponsors to back him, it looked like that dream would never come true. While his first attempt at the Busch Series failed miserably, Park returned to modified racing where he turned in a number of respectable finishes on the track.

Then he got a message on his answering machine one day in 1996. The caller said he was Dale Earnhardt . . . and he was looking for Steve Park. Park ignored the message – he had friends who liked to play practical jokes like this!

Earnhardt called back and left another message, but Park still didn't return the call. It was only after his mom, who was an Earnhardt fan, listened to the recording and said, "That's him . . . I know his voice, and that's him," that he called the number left by "Dale." Still skeptical, Park was connected to Ty Norris, the Earnhardt team manager who said, according to Park, "Hey, buddy, we've been trying to get a hold of you for a while." Park was offered a driving position on the Earnhardt Busch team.

Dale gives Steve Park some advice before a race.

John Cordes/ICON SMI

Earnhardt had faith in his new recruit. "This kid is good, or we wouldn't have him where he is today," said Earnhardt of Park. "He's got a lot of learning to do, but he wants to win, and that's why he's with us." And Park did his best not to disappoint his mentor. Park handed in the best season ever for a Busch Series rookie in his freshman year and then moved to Winston Cup, where he continues to dominate the field with teammate Dale Earnhardt Jr. beside him. You can learn more about Park at his official Internet web site (*www.steve-park.com*).

Steve's Only Regret

"The only bad thing about that phone call (from Dale Earnhardt) now is that I have always prided myself on having a state-of-the-art digital answering machine," said Steve Park about his fateful call from Earnhardt." But you couldn't save the message because of the computer chip. I'd love to have that answering machine message."

Michael Waltrip

The new kid in the pits at DEI is Michael Waltrip,

who was introduced in the fall of 2000 to the team and employees of Earnhardt's garage in Mooresville with these words: "Since 1997, every driver of every car in every division that DEI entered has won a race," team manager Ty Norris said. "We wouldn't be standing here with Michael Waltrip if we didn't think that trend is going to continue."

Considering Waltrip's winless streak (failing to reach the finish line first in over 450 Winston Cup starts) combined with his brother Darrell's NASCAR success, that was *a lot* of pressure! Many in the press and on the racing circuit were ready to consider Waltrip a driver who had missed out on his opportunity. But Waltrip saw Earnhardt's backing as a way to show what he was capable of doing. "Earnhardt is a fierce competitor that believes there's nothing good about second place," he said. "I can't wait to work with these guys . . . They've won races and championships and that's what I want to do, win races and bring another championship to NAPA and DEI."

And Earnhardt believed in his latest addition to the garage. "I've always believed Michael could drive a race car," he said. "I think if you put the right resources behind him, he can win races and will win races, and better win races."

Although Waltrip won the 2001 Daytona 500 – his first win in 15 years and in 463 Winston Cup starts – the tragic death of his good friend and boss will always cloud the victory. After all, Waltrip said, "The only reason I won this race is Dale Earnhardt."

Dale (right) and Michael Waltrip speak to the press about their partnership.

Memorabilia Mayhem

On February 19, 2001, NASCAR stores all across North America had their busiest day in years. Fans and collectors swamped the stores in search of all the Dale Earnhardt merchandise they could carry – hats, mugs, T-shirts, die-cast cars and more. Anything with Earnhardt's name, number or signature on it was a hot seller. It wasn't uncommon for stores to sell out of Earnhardt merchandise within an hour of opening, and some sold out even sooner.

> "If they had $1,000 worth of this stuff, I would have bought $1,000 worth of it. And I'm not planning to sell any of it. He was my man."
>
> — An Earnhardt fan on buying collectibles

Bob Swan, a retailer in Tannersville, Pennsylvania, told a reporter that when he went to open his store the day after the crash, there were 15 people waiting for him, eager to get inside and start buying up Earnhardt merchandise. "As I look around, there's hardly anything left," he remarked. "You name it, if it had 'Earnhardt' on it, it sold. They just wiped me out."

What color belt would you pair with this belt buckle? Black, of course!

It wasn't limited to the stores, either. The Internet teemed with fans of The Intimidator, intent on owning souvenirs of their favorite driver, no matter what the cost. Three days before Earnhardt's death, an Earnhardt Jebco clock went up for bid on *Ebay.com,* starting at $10. Five days later, the bid was $255.99.

Time the performance of your favorite NASCAR driver with an Earnhardt clock.

On-line retailer Bryan Miller of *prosportsmemora-bilia.com* reported that he sold his entire stock of Earnhardt photos in the hours after the crash. "As soon as something like this happens," he said, "items can sell out instantly."

It was almost as if Earnhardt's fans were trying to find anything connected with him now that he was gone. A "feeding frenzy" is how one retailer described how his customers reacted. "They're grabbing up everything," said another.

But Earnhardt's popularity had made his name and merchandise famous for years before that fateful day at Daytona. In fact, Earnhardt and his products did more to make NASCAR a household word than any other driver in history. During his lifetime, Earnhardt merchandise out-sold that of nearly all the other drivers on the NASCAR circuit – combined! It's reported that Earnhardt merchandise alone accounted for half of NASCAR's licensed product sales. Fans and collectors have had to set apart entire rooms in their homes to accommodate all their Intimidator merchandise. Earnhardt's image, car, signature or even that stylized #3

What better way to remember such a "fiery" individual than with an Earnhardt lighter.

graced everything from die-cast cars to fishing lures and just about everything in between.

Since Earnhardt's tragic death, many fans have been prompting NASCAR to retire the #3, or at least give it to Dale Jr. No matter what they do with the number, no other driver will ever be able to give it as much honor as The Intimidator. Dale Earnhardt certainly didn't own the copyright to the number 3, but the digit belonged to him in the hearts and minds of fans everywhere. Sometimes the stylized #3 was all it took to turn an ordinary item into a piece of Earnhardt merchandise. A window sticker of his distinctive number could turn any car into a rolling tribute to The Man In Black.

Cars

When race fans tune in to Talladega or take a seat at Dover Downs, they don't do it just to see their favorite drivers try for the checkered flag. The cars are just as colorful as the drivers who build and race them, and Earnhardt's long career is the tale of many different vehicles. So one of the most popular items fans purchased to show their loyalty to The Intimidator was die-cast cars, replicas of the many machines that carried Earnhardt to Victory Lane over the years. Those cars represent a lot of years, going back long before Earnhardt made NASCAR a household name. Even back to the 1956 Ford Victoria (in pink, believe it or not) on which Earnhardt cut his racing teeth at the ripe old age of 18!

Just about every car Earnhardt ever raced had an accompanying die-cast replica made in honor of it. The Dodge Charger and the Chevy

Two die-cast cars represent the vehicles that have carried Earnhardt to victory.

Malibus he raced back in the 1970s, the Ford Thunderbirds and Chevrolet Monte Carlos that Wrangler sponsored through the 1980s and those sleek black Monte Carlos that won Earnhardt his Winston Cups could be found on store shelves and collector's desks everywhere. The special paint schemes from such sponsors as Bass Pro Shops, Coca-Cola and the 1996 Olympics also made their way into die-cast form.

No matter what size, from the 1:64 Matchbox-sized toys to the 1:24 collector's items, Earnhardt's die-cast cars let the fans commemorate their favorite driver's memorable races of a long and honorable career. Of course, you need more than a car to make your NASCAR dreams come true, and the die-cast phenomenon covers all the bases with other items, like pit wagons and gas pumps.

Keep Dale's legacy alive with one of the many Earnhardt T-shirts on the market.

Apparel

During Earnhardt's lengthy career, you could always see people of various ages and genders showing off their support for The Man In Black. Turn on the TV during a race day, and you'd see more #3 T-shirts in the crowd than you could count. Fans could warm up at the track with Earnhardt jackets and sweatshirts.

But Earnhardt apparel didn't stop there. You could find ties, pajamas, boxer shorts and even baby shoes emblazoned with that stylized #3. For the die-hard fans, reproductions of The Intimidator's racing uniform could even be purchased. It seemed that no matter your age or profession, you could show off your support for The Intimidator with a wide array of clothes and accessories. After all, that's how fans recognize each other at the race!

Sponsors

Earnhardt's career saw a lot of sponsors over the years, and those sponsors inspired a number of other items for the fans to collect. When Dale picked up Coca-Cola as a sponsor, thirsty fans could fill their shelves with collectible bottles featuring the "Coca-Cola Racing Family," with

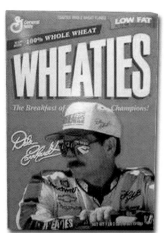

Earnhardt as a proud member. Sun-drop soda (found mostly in the southeastern United States) paid tribute to Earnhardt in 1986, with a series of collectible bottles. For fans who liked a good breakfast before heading for the track, Earnhardt's tie-in with the Kellogg Company opened the door for a number of cereal boxes, too.

Dale Earnhardt reinforces the fact that Wheaties is the "breakfast of champions"!

Outdoorsy Stuff

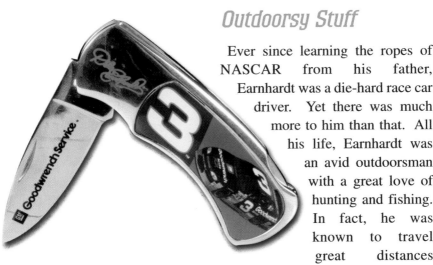

Ever since learning the ropes of NASCAR from his father, Earnhardt was a die-hard race car driver. Yet there was much more to him than that. All his life, Earnhardt was an avid outdoorsman with a great love of hunting and fishing. In fact, he was known to travel great distances around the country just to pursue his love of the sport!

Earnhardt was an avid hunter and outdoorsman, and probably kept a knife just like this one in his pocket.

Any Earnhardt fan who shares The Intimidator's fondness for the great outdoors can celebrate his memory with accessories for hunting and camping. Frost Cutlery and Case Knives, two leading names in the knife business, produced a number of commemorative knives to honor Earnhardt's life and career. The sizes included 3" pocket knives, 4" lock-backs and a gorgeous 12" Bowie knife. By the way, that last one can be worth a lot of money, so we wouldn't recommend using it to clean a deer on your next hunting trip. Putting it on display would be much better!

Driving Like Dale

If you can't slide into the passenger seat of Dale's #3 Chevy, you can at least take the wheel – of a 1:12 scale version of his 2000 Goodwrench Plus car! This remote-controlled speedster can travel at speeds up to 20 miles per hour, and is capable of taking on the fiercest of competitors. Let the race begin!

For fans who preferred the peace and tranquility of fishing over the rugged action of hunting, there was even an Earnhardt fishing lure produced with his likeness. After all, one of Earnhardt's many sponsors was Bass Pro Shops, and what better way is there to honor a lifelong fisherman?

Cards Of Every Kind

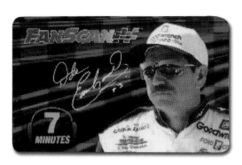

If you can't just hop on your private Learjet to visit friends like Earnhardt did, you can at least call them with an Earnhardt pre-paid phone card.

Dale Earnhardt's image graced many different kinds of collectible cards.

When NASCAR racing had finally established itself as a major sporting event (thanks, in no small part, to Earnhardt), the market for NASCAR trading cards exploded. Since the early 1990s, companies like Upper Deck, Press Pass and Pinnacle have churned out thousands of cards for the sport, and Earnhardt himself was featured on literally hundreds of them.

Beginning in 1995, Earnhardt even turned up on a number of phone cards, which were randomly distributed in trading card packs around the country (just in case you wanted to give The Man In Black a friendly call). But if you don't have the patience to sort through several packs of cards looking for that phone card, you can just pop down to your local gas station or convenience store – chances are they might carry Earnhardt calling cards as well.

Games

Sadly, race cars only have one seat. So fans couldn't very well be able to go for a ride with Earnhardt – that is, not until the advent of such computer games as NASCAR 2001 from Playstation, where you could

Race around the game board playing
Dale Earnhardt Monopoly!

race against other drivers as The Intimidator, or, if you were brave enough, race against him and hope he wouldn't screech past you and leave you in the dust! For the low-tech Earnhardt fan, you could even find out what it was like to own a racing empire with the amazing Dale Earnhardt edition of Monopoly. Players could race around the square track of the board, trade Earnhardt cars and build race shops and track garages (instead of the usual houses and hotels). With a little luck, they could even end up owning Earnhardt's jet – well, at least in game form!

A Dale Earnhardt Christmas tree ornament is the perfect addition to your yule.

If you are a little more mechanically inclined, perhaps you'd like to build your own version of one of Earnhardt's cars, just like a member of the pit crew! There are many different Earnhardt model cars on the market just waiting for you to try your hand at them.

And So Much More!

There are items on the market that no one would ever think to associate with a sport like NASCAR. Who could link holidays or cuddly plush toys with a sport that involves high-speed thrills? Nevertheless, NASCAR and Earnhardt made their influence felt in such corners, with

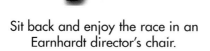

collectible Christmas tree ornaments, adorable teddy bears and even sporty golf equipment.

Try as he might, for 20 years, Earnhardt only conquered the Daytona 500 once. But his fans will never forget the immortal day of February 15, 1998, when The Man In Black roared into first place and took the checkered flag – and unintentionally created a whole new souvenir. Following his triumph, Earnhardt celebrated by zooming into the infield and tearing up the grass with victory doughnuts. Long after the race's end, worshippers of The Intimidator swarmed onto the knoll, intent on taking home chunks of sod that his Monte Carlo's tires had shredded. The fans will always remember that day, although Daytona's groundskeepers may have liked to forget it!

Sit back and enjoy the race in an Earnhardt director's chair.

It's Race Day!

Picture this scenario: You lean back in your #3 director's chair, and use an Earnhardt bottle opener to pop open a collector's bottle of Coke, which you pour into an Earnhardt glass mug. You grab a bag of chips and dump them onto your Dale Earnhardt collector's plate. You check your Earnhardt watch to make sure it's the right time to turn on the television set, and now you're finally ready to settle yourself in for an afternoon of watching the latest

Earnhardt's name appeared on many items, including soda bottles.

NASCAR race, and anxiously wait for The Man In Black to take home that elusive eighth Winston Cup,

Sadly, Dale Earnhardt never got that chance. But in the hearts and minds of true race fans around the globe, Earnhardt will always be the serious, determined driver who put a whole new and modern face on NASCAR racing. He changed the sport's image from that of broken-down cars speeding around Southern backwater tracks into a nationally popular televised event.

In the process, he made the act of being Dale Earnhardt into a full-time occupation. His name and image graced so many diverse products that it became unbelievably difficult to keep track of them all. And his exposure made people nationwide

Dale was a man of action – so collecting action figures in honor of him is only natural!

take notice of the sport he loved. Ask anyone about NASCAR, and they might have never heard of Mark Martin or Bobby Labonte, but everyone knew who Dale Earnhardt was. With so much merchandise around, it was impossible not to!

The Torch
Passes

Passing The Torch To Dale Earnhardt Jr.

Some families are destined to live out their dreams, and the Earnhardt family is one of them. Three generations of Earnhardts have felt the thrill of sitting in the driver's seat of a race car, experiencing the rush of adrenaline while passing a speeding vehicle. Like his grandfather and his father, Dale Earnhardt Jr. always knew that racing was in his blood.

Dale Jr.'s father was given the nickname – The Intimidator – that described his willingness to do whatever it took to reach the finish line. As they say, like father, like son.

Dale Jr., born on October 10, 1974, in Kannapolis, North Carolina, has been branded The Imitator, a nickname that glorifies the fact that he is a chip off of the old block. But how different is Dale Jr. from his father? How did the young driver discover the world of racing? And what's next for Dale Jr., the budding star who has the potential to fulfill the amazing Earnhardt legacy?

Dale Earnhardt Jr. follows in the footsteps of his father Dale and grandfather Ralph.

A Third Generation Of Racing

Like his dad, Dale Jr. picked up the passion for racing at a young age. When he was around 10 or 11 years old, the elder Dale and his wife, Teresa, took their son to a go-kart track. His parents watched him drive his car around the track, until suddenly his go-kart was clipped and went soaring through the air. When Dale Sr. ran to see whether Dale Jr. was hurt, he discovered something interesting – the child's main concern wasn't his own well-being, but that of the car. At this point, Dale Sr. believed his son would follow his career path and he began making plans to steer him in the right direction.

Dale Earnhardt Jr. shares a lighthearted moment with Mark Martin.

The Race Begins

In 1994, young Dale's career began at such tracks as South Carolina's Florence Motor Speedway, Myrtle Beach Speedway, Nashville Speedway USA and Tri-County Speedway in North Carolina. He raced in the NASCAR Weekly Racing Series and, he was victorious in three races. He also took 12 poles and made 113 starts. In 1996, he qualified seventh and finished 13th in his first Busch Series start at Myrtle Beach. But that was nothing compared to what he would yet accomplish.

It all began with taking his own initiative. Dale Jr., or "Little E," as he is often called, talks about his early relationship with his father. "I hardly ever saw him, because he was always traveling." And also of his earliest lessons, "I learned by watching TV, or going to races and seeing how they do it."

However, Dale Sr. was not going to let his son wander around blindly in the dark. Seeing Dale Jr. stumble through a few lackluster seasons in the Busch Series in 1996 and 1997, the elder Earnhardt stepped in and gave his son his very own Busch car to drive. Those around him, including his crew chief Tony Eury, questioned his judgement. "Everybody looked at us like we were crazy. They said there ain't no way we could take that kid and win a championship."

A Son Speaks About His Father

"His friendship is the greatest gift you could ever obtain. Out of all his attributes, it is the most impressive."

On The Right Track

And Little E proved them all wrong! The Generation X race driver picked up a Busch championship, and Eury said after working with Dale Jr. that he "learned faster than anybody I've ever worked with." Dale Jr. credits his success to having such a great car, and his belief in himself. He felt ready to win the championship – and he went on to win another Busch championship the following year. With many fans, hype and publicity surrounding him, Dale Jr. entered the NASCAR Winston Cup as a rookie in 2000 with the highest of expectations.

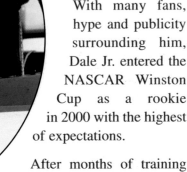

Dale Earnhardt Jr. stares out from behind the wheel.

John Cordes/ICON SMI

After months of training and sheer determination, Dale Jr. started the season out well. In fact, during the DirecTV 500 at Texas Motor Speedway in April of 1998, he made his first trip to Victory Lane in just his 12th Winston Cup race! Placing seventh, his father was very pleased. Dale Jr. told the press after the race that "[my father] told me that he loved me and then he said he just wanted to make sure I took the time to enjoy this and realize what we accomplished today. That was pretty cool on his part to be thinking about that at that particular time. This was a product of his work. He's proud of his son, but he's also proud that he built this team and the team won the race."

Fatherly Advice

Dale has said that his father has given him good advice on "all kinds of things, but mainly the average fatherly advice, like staying away from drugs, irresponsible drinking. As far as the track there is not one key piece of advice."

After the race, Dale Sr., told a reporter, "I'll tell you, he's something else. He was talking about coming to Texas and winning his first Winston Cup race. I knew the kid could do it. This kid has worked hard, had a good car and drove a good race." This was a victory that father and son had accomplished, together.

Dale Jr. put out a respectable performance during the rest of his freshman year in Winston Cup – he had 19 top-20 finishes and two victories under his belt by the end of the season. Unfortunately, he also faced fierce competition for the Raybestos Rookie of the Year Award, which ultimately went to Matt Kenseth.

John Cordes/ICON SMI

Dale Earnhardt Jr. has seen success on both the Busch and Winston Cup racing circuits. Is a Winston Cup championship next?

Ferocity Runs In The Family

There were physical differences between father and son – Dale Jr. had no moustache, or frown, and in fact, was thought of as a "dreamer" by his father. But they certainly shared one common trait – their ability to perform on the track. On several occasions, father and son raced each other, and Dale Jr. admitted to his competitive streak. "Sure, I'd like to beat him," Dale answered to early inquiries about whether he would like to beat his legendary father in a race, "but I'd like to beat them all."

In November 1998, during an exhibition race in Japan, Dale Jr. did indeed accomplish the feat of crossing the finish line before his father – finishing sixth while his father finished eighth. The crowd went wild when son nudged father halfway through the race, giving The Intimidator a taste of his own medicine. Dale Jr. made light of the incident, though. "It was a bump, just tapped him a little bit, that's it," Little E said. "No big deal. No family dispute came out of it."

Dale Jr. outran his father at the DirecTV 500, earning his first Winston Cup win in 2000.

In an interview in 2000, Dale Jr. had this to say about the father-son competition. "When I first started competing against [my dad], it was really fun. Now it's kind of wearing off; he's just another guy. But when you beat him, it kind of makes the ride home uncomfortable. I mean, it doesn't matter to me whether I beat him or not. He beat me so many damn times at everything for so many years I got kind of used to it. In Japan, that first race with him, I had to beat him there. But from here on out, he can beat me as many times as he wants."

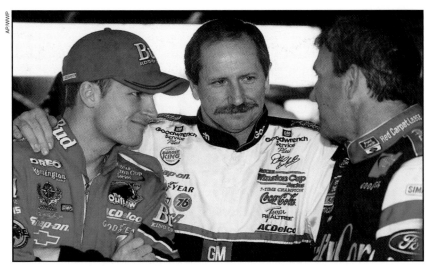

AP/WWP

The three Dales (Dale Jr., Dale Sr. and Dale Jarrett) talk
before the start of the 2000 Daytona 500.

NASCAR's Sexiest Man Alive

Dale Jr.'s popularity has soared in recent years. Female fans swoon over the handsome driver, who has helped bring the Generation X crowd to the world of NASCAR. The young star has made several public appearances. MTV did a "True Life" documentary on the life of a race car driver with young Dale as the star. He also appeared in *PEOPLE* magazine's "Sexiest Men" issue in November, 2000 as one of NASCAR's sexiest drivers.

Yet Dale is very modest. "I don't see myself as popular," Dale Jr. has said. "I think when a race fan comes to get an autograph, it's just a novelty. I think the popularity stems from Budweiser, NASCAR, this car being in an odd place and causing this much attention."

Dale Jr., aside from winning more races, has said that in his spare time he would like to travel – go to Hawaii, Australia, and Europe. He enjoys interacting with his fans and can often be found at autograph sessions or serving as a guest on on-line chats. He also likes water sports and playing around with computers. In addition, Dale Jr. is a great fan of music – rap music and Elvis are a few of his favorites. He also writes poetry. In fact, one of the poems he wrote was transformed into a song and performed by his friends' band, Bridge.

Dale Jr. definitely wants to be remembered for his racing, and would like to be considered one of the best auto racers of all time. However, he would also like to be considered one of the more entertaining or interesting drivers, on the track as well as off. "I just want to be considered as entertaining, honest and genuine. It's going to be hard to be considered one of the best because the best have been so good."

Dale Jr. is a fan favorite because of his good looks and awesome skills.

Daytona 500

Always moving ahead, Dale Jr. had high hopes for the 2001 Daytona 500, his second start in the event often touted as the Super Bowl of auto racing. "I'm pretty confident that I'm going to win the Daytona 500 this year, because I dreamed about it. You can call me crazy, but I'll be talking to you at the post-race interview, talking about how I did it."

He was also thrilled at the prospect of racing with his father. "This is a rare sport where father and son can run together and be competitors at the same time and be successful."

And what was he looking forward to the most about racing with his very own dad? In another interview, Dale Jr. confesses, "It most certainly is fun [to pass my dad on the racetrack]. It's a big deal when I pass him. He acts like it's not a big deal, but I enjoy it. If I see him ahead on a racetrack, I try not to get too excited. It's hard sometimes, but you want to race with him because you never know how many opportunities you'll get."

Dale Jr's Role Models

Dale admits that his favorite drivers growing up (other than his father) were Darrell Waltrip, David Pearson, Bobby Allison and Jimmy Means.

Although Dale Jr.'s dreams of winning the Daytona 500 did not come true, the event should have still been a triumph for Dale Jr. – he was running in second place, directly behind fellow teammate Michael Waltrip and directly in front of his father. But then came the crash that marred the day's celebration – and will surely have a lasting impact on Dale Jr.'s life. His father was dead.

Moving On

Although Dale Jr. took the loss of his father especially hard, he has kept a stiff upper lip in the days immediately following the accident.

"Everybody deals with this," he had told the press. "We're making our way and we appreciate everybody's support. I mean it really, really means a lot. It makes a big difference when you see the reaction from hundreds and hundreds of people like we have already. You know, we appreciate everybody's support and it's a tough time."

Dale Jr. could use an extra hand as he signs autographs for his many fans.

Though still getting over the loss of his father, Dale Jr. has not stopped racing – and raced in NASCAR's Dura-Lube 400, the following week on February 25th. "I'm sure he'd want us to keep going so that's what we're going to do," Dale Jr. explained. Unfortunately, in an eerie coincidence, Dale Jr.'s car slammed into a wall, but luckily the young driver was able to walk away from the crash.

And does Dale ever hope that he will be seen as the kind of star competitor that his father was? "I hope so," Dale has said. "Those type of things take time. It's going to take a long time."

Dale Jr.'s #8 has a chance to become as legendary
a number as his father's famous #3.

His career shaped and shadowed by his father, Dale Jr. successfully moved in his own path, with his father's support and advice. With this tragic loss, each victory for The Imitator is a reminder of the great Intimidator's love of racing and remarkable career. As the torch passes on, and the Earnhardt tradition of racing continues, he will continue to remind racing fans that he, like his father, has the potential to be one of the best.

Thanks For The Memories

The Racing World
Remembers Dale Earnhardt®

The loss of The Intimidator cast a pall over the entire racing world and many people wondered whether NASCAR would or could go on. Would they race the next week at Rockingham? Would NASCAR ever be the same?

In the midst of it all, Dale Jr., the heir-apparent, stayed strong. "We'll get through this," he said to a television station in his native North Carolina the day after the tragedy. "I'm sure he'd want us to keep going, and that's what we're going to do."

Wesley Hitt/Icon SMI

Like father, like son: Dale Earnhardt and Dale Earnhardt Jr.

All Of NASCAR® Feels The Loss

Bill France, chairman of the board of NASCAR, spoke at a somber press conference the day after the tragedy. "This is a tough period in NASCAR's history," he said. "I can't think of any time that has been more tough. Dale was really a booster of NASCAR. Whenever you asked him to do something to promote the series, he stood tall."

AP/WWP

Driver Bobby Labonte talks with NASCAR
President Mike Helton at Daytona.

When France was asked about how NASCAR would be able to fill the void left by Earnhardt's passing, he admitted, "It's going to take time, if we ever fill it. I'm sure we will. Life has to go on."

The feeling of loss was shared by Mike Helton, president of NASCAR, at the same press conference. "It's just hard to comprehend the statistic sheets for Dale Earnhardt are now permanent," said Helton. "But it's really easy to understand that Dale Earnhardt will be a part of this sport for many generations to come."

A Bittersweet Victory

The entire NASCAR community was united in sorrow by Earnhardt's untimely death, but race winner Michael Waltrip endured a particularly harsh roller coaster of emotions – having achieved his first Winston Cup victory in 463 attempts, only to discover that moments before he crossed the finish line his car owner Earnhardt had hit the wall.

"Yesterday was our day," recounted Waltrip the Monday after the race. "I had won the race and I was telling everybody about it and I just couldn't wait until I got that big grab on my neck and a big hug [from Earnhardt]. I just knew any minute Dale was going to run into Victory Lane and say 'That's what I'm talking about right there.' But that wasn't to be.

"My belief is that in a twinkle of an eye you're in the presence of the Lord. So instead of patting me in the back and hugging me, he's up there hanging out with my dad. So that ain't a bad thing, either."

The Accident

In the aftermath of the tragedy, many fans directed their anger toward driver Sterling Marlin, who had bumped Earnhardt in the final lap. Marlin responded by saying, "A lot of people can hide behind names and say a lot of things on the Internet that are not true. Maybe it's just people that are frustrated and looking for somebody to blame. I think it was just purely a racing accident."

Sterling Marlin has had to deal with fans angry over the loss of Dale Earnhardt.

AP/WWP

He also said about Earnhardt's death, "It shocked me. We didn't know it was that bad. Tony Glover [Marlin's team manager] told me about the time we were getting ready to leave the race track in Daytona that it didn't look good for Earnhardt.

"I said, 'Well, what do you mean?' He said, 'He's hurt pretty bad.' By the time we got to the airport, they came and told us. I was in total shock. It made you just want to go throw up, just sick at your stomach. You couldn't believe it could happen."

> "Dale was my friend. We hunted and raced together. We laughed and cried together. We were able to work side-by-side and have the success we had for almost 20 years because we were friends first. I will miss him always. He was the greatest."
>
> — Richard Childress remembers

Michael Waltrip defended Marlin in a press conference. "I ask that everyone keep Sterling Marlin in their prayers," said Waltrip. "Sterling didn't do anything wrong. Sterling was simply racing. When the checkered's waving, nobody is going to let off. When they rubbed, I'm sure Sterling didn't think Dale would wreck."

Driver Ken Schrader, who was also involved in Earnhardt's fatal crash, discussed the moments right after the crash in an interview with *The Kansas City Star.* "I saw that I was OK to get out [of the car]. Dale's car is right there. I went up to his window to talk to him . . . I don't really want to go into what I saw, but I had grave concerns right then.

> "We tended to believe he was a little bit invincible and he had shown us over the years there was no reason to believe he wasn't. Reality does catch up with us."
>
> — Fellow Winston Cup driver Ken Schrader

"I didn't think it was that type of hit," Schrader continued. "I was caught off guard [by the tragic severity of Earnhardt's injuries]. We've all taken harder hits."

The Last Cowboy

AP/WWP

Kyle Petty lost his son Adam in a crash at New Hampshire International Speedway in 2000.

One legendary NASCAR family that could personally relate to this grief was the Pettys. Adam Petty, the celebrated grandson of racing icon Richard Petty and son of current Winston Cup driver Kyle Petty, had recently died in a horrible crash at the New Hampshire International Speedway in 2000.

Kyle Petty spoke in awe of his racing contemporary, "When [Earnhardt] was at the top of his game, he was amazing. He could do things with a race car that you didn't think anybody could do. There was a time when you could see a 20-car pileup and, if just one car made it through, it was the one Earnhardt was driving.

"For a lot of fans, Dale Earnhardt was what they thought about when they thought about NASCAR racing," Petty said. "He could do so much and was so talented. He knew it, and he knew you knew it. That grin of his, a lot of times you wouldn't know what he was thinking but you thought you did. And it might not mean a thing in the world, but he knew you were trying to figure it out. He was the last cowboy."

NASCAR® Drivers React

The 2001 Daytona 500 was also marked by another dramatic accident with about 25 laps to go. Tony Stewart's Home Depot car wound up airborne in the midst of an accident that involved 19 cars, knocking many of the race's highest-profile drivers out of the race before the stretch run. Despite the spectacular crash, no drivers were seriously injured in the accident.

Tony Stewart is one of several younger NASCAR drivers who follows in The Intimidator's footsteps.

Stewart released a statement regarding Earnhardt after the race. "Dale Earnhardt made a difference in the world," he said. "On the track, he made us all better drivers because he set a standard of excellence we all aspired to achieve. He had a passion and a desire that took the sport of NASCAR to a new level every time he climbed in the car. Off the track he was a kind, giving, loving man who gave his all to his family and friends. I did not know him as long as most of the other drivers but he made a huge impact on my life in the years I have been in NASCAR. I am grateful and blessed to have had the benefit of his wisdom and guidance."

Rusty Wallace and his family took Earnhardt's death very hard. "Patti [Rusty's wife] and I are both having a hard time dealing with this," said Wallace, who narrowly edged Earnhardt for the Winston Cup championship in 1989. "It's such a tragic loss. We're grieving just like so many people are today with such a loss. We've had some helluva battles out there on the race track through the years, but we've had so many good times off the track. God only created one Dale Earnhardt and no one will ever replace him, neither in our sport or in our hearts."

AP/WWP

Rusty Wallace had been one of Dale Earnhardt's oldest rivals.

Champions Recall A Champion

Among the many things that Earnhardt will always be remembered for, one will always ring loud and true – champion – as in seven-time Winston Cup champion.

Dale Jarrett, the 1999 champion, remembered his friend and rival: "As millions of race fans mourn the loss of the man they knew as The Intimidator, the sport and the race that he truly loved has taken from me one of my best friends," he said. "I know I should feel fortunate that I had the opportunity to race with, tangle with, sometimes outrun and, like most, usually finish behind, the greatest driving talent NASCAR racing has ever seen. Just know Dale that we love you and we all are truly going to miss you. Thanks for making our sport what it is today and for being my friend."

Not content to rest on his laurels, Earnhardt had mounted a campaign for what would have been a record-breaking eighth title during the 2000 season. Eventual champion Bobby Labonte said, "I, like everyone else, am in shock with the passing of Dale Earnhardt. Besides being an incredible driver and spokesman for the sport he so loved, he was a true friend

> "Dale Earnhardt was the greatest race driver who ever lived. It's a tremendous loss for the sport. I've said this many times over the years, if there was ever a natural-born race-car driver, he was it."
>
> — Retired NASCAR legend Ned Jarrett

and has been a major influence on my life and career. Understandably, my family's thoughts are with Teresa, Kerry, Kelly, Dale Jr. and Taylor Nicole as well as all of the employees and their families at Richard Childress Racing and Dale Earnhardt Incorporated. May God bless all of them and watch over them in this time of need."

Dale Remembered As A Fierce Competitor

"I've got so many Dale Earnhardt stories I could write a book," driver Jimmy Spencer said. "That 3 car scared every driver, because they knew what was coming. Dale Earnhardt never gave up. He didn't care if he was five laps down; you were going to have to work to get past him. He would race you just as hard for 20th as he would for the win, and as competitors we all realized that and expected that from him."

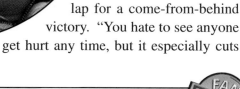

Jimmy Spencer was familiar with Dale Earnhardt's intimidating presence on the track.

Wesley Hitt/Icon SMI

Driver Jeremy Mayfield was involved in a classic encounter with Earnhardt at a 2000 race at Pocono Raceway, where Mayfield gave The Man In Black a taste of his own medicine by bumping him on the final lap for a come-from-behind victory. "You hate to see anyone get hurt any time, but it especially cuts deep since it's Earnhardt." Mayfield said in a press statement on his Internet web site. "The guy is a master. He's been doing this for years and he's been doing it better than anybody. One of the biggest thrills of my career was the deal last year at Pocono. You know he never said anything to me about that? He came over and gave me that grin of his, and that was like his seal of approval."

"We can't replace Dale Earnhardt. This is the worst thing – this is the biggest thing that's happened to this sport since I've been in it. Dale Earnhardt is known all over the world. This is like when John Kennedy got shot, or when Martin Luther King got shot. This is a day that we will remember for the rest of our lives."

— Friend and former NASCAR competitor Darrell Waltrip

Rivals On The Track

Even Earnhardt's rivals were in awe of his abilities. His on-track rivalry with Jeff Gordon will become a permanent part of racing lore.

"[My wife] Brooke and I are deeply saddened by this devastating loss," Gordon said in a press release following the tragedy. "Not only is

Jeff Gordon tangled with Dale Earnhardt
several times on the racetrack.

it a huge loss for this sport, but a huge loss for me personally. Dale taught me so much and became a great friend."

"I will tell you that some of the fiercest and most successful drivers are also the most aggravating on the track," said driver Mark Martin. "Dale was incredibly tenacious; he drove me to rise to his level. He made me want to be the best, because he made me want to beat him. I have never in all of my experience raced against any-one with as much desire to win as he had, and that's saying a lot, because I've raced against them all. It's just so tragic. He was so much to so many. He's left a giant, dark, black hole behind him. He will be missed by millions."

Jeff Burton battled Earnhardt and Labonte for the 2000 Winston Cup championship, ultimately finishing third in the overall points standings. "He [was] tough as hell on the track," recalled Burton. "He never gave anything, but you always knew what to expect, and he had a lot of respect for it, because he treated everyone equally. He was really frustrating to drive against, because there were times when he could have made it much easier, but that wasn't in his personality. You always had to work that much harder with him.

Jeff Burton was one of Earnhardt's competitors in the drive for the 2000 Winston Cup.

"The guy was the ambassador for our sport, our leader, our trendset-ter. It's just a huge loss to our commu-nity; he was a huge influence on so many people."

The Generosity Of Earnhardt

Driver John Andretti relayed a story that showed that the The Man In Black had a side that people may not have known about. "The thing I remember most about Dale Earnhardt – and the thing that, to me, really epitomizes him – is something that happened at Talladega my rookie sea-son [1994]. The second race there, my team [Billy Hagan] just did not have a lot of money. We had one good restrictor plate engine and we broke it in practice. There was no way we were even going to make the race.

"I was walking through the garage before second-round qualifying and ran into Richard Childress. He said, 'How are things going?' and I said, 'Not so good.' I told him what was going on but didn't say much more. Even if I had thought to ask him for some help there is no way we could have afforded anything.

"I found out later he told Earnhardt about it and Earnhardt had an idea. He and Richard gave one of their qualifying engines to Dave Marcis, and had Marcis move his qualifying engine to our car. The engine we got was phenomenal. We were 11th fastest in second-round qualifying and made the race because of Dale Earnhardt and Richard Childress.

> "There's been a Dale Earnhardt as long as I can remember, not just racing but racing and winning. For the younger guys in the sport, he has been our Richard Petty. He was the guy who won all of the championships. I'll miss him on the track, I'll miss him in the garage. Our sport is going to miss him a lot."
>
> — Driver Jeremy Mayfield

AP/WWP

Jeremy Mayfield (#12) bested his idol
Dale Earnhardt in the Pocono 500.

"They never asked for anything and they never even told anybody, as far as I know. Dale and Richard helped us out because we needed help. We didn't have the money to pay for it, and they knew that, but they helped us out anyway.

"There are a lot of stories like that about Earnhardt. He helped a lot of people, and no one ever knew."

NASCAR® Legends Pay Tribute To Earnhardt

Dale Earnhardt is flanked by singer Anita Cochran and owner Richard Childress.

APWWP

In the wake of Earnhardt's death, retired NASCAR greats also paid their heartfelt respects.

Retired racer A.J. Foyt said, "My heart goes out to his family because they are the ones who suffer most. Racing lost one of the greatest stock car drivers that ever lived and I lost a great friend."

Darrell Waltrip, a NASCAR great who retired at the end of the 2000 season, was calling the race for Fox Sports when Earnhardt died. Darrell, the older brother of Daytona winner Michael Waltrip, appeared on the *Larry King Live* show the day after the accident.

"[Dale] was exciting on the track, and he had a lot of fans. Even people who didn't pull for him were amazed with what he could do with a race car."

— Winston Cup driver Joe Nemechek

"I loved Dale Earnhardt; he was a good friend," he told King during the broadcast. "There were times I wanted to grab him and shake him and ask him what was he thinking and what was he doing. But the man had a side to him. He was one guy on the racetrack, when he put that helmet on he was somebody else, but when he took it off, he was Dale Earnhardt, and he was as gentle as they come. He was a gentle giant."

King asked Waltrip the age-old question – when tragedies like this happen, why would drivers continue to race?

"You know, why do farmers have a drought and lose their crops and go back and plant them all over again?" asked Waltrip. "Why do airplanes fall out of sky? [We've] got to get to where we are going, [so] we get back on an airplane.

"But I think, for me and for others like me, it's the love of the game, it's that passion we have. We can't quit. We're in it to the bitter end or we're in it to the sweet end, and you just never know in a game like this how it's going to turn out."

Bill Shipley/Icon SMI

Michael Waltrip was the winner of the 2001 Daytona 500.

The Fans Speak Out

On February 18, 2001, the world of NASCAR lost one of its icons. Dale Earnhardt was not just any guy behind the wheel of the #3 Black Monte Carlo, he was a man of the people. For his fans, he was one of the their family. As Randy Fultz of Bloomington, Indiana, told reporters, "We probably know more about Dale Earnhardt than we do about people in our own family."

The Final Lap

News of Earnhardt's death rocked the world. Fans had seen the race car driver face close calls before and this one didn't look that much different. He was The Intimidator – nothing, no one could stop him. *The Dallas Morning News* reported, "He was supposed to be too relentless, too tenacious, too mean to die. He was supposed to ram his car right into death's right-rear bumper and barrel through its outstretched hands."

But on February 18, the events that occurred on turn 4 at Daytona were too much for even The Intimidator, and for his fans, things will never be the same. One fan commented that while people will always ask, "'Where were you when you heard JFK was shot?' NASCAR fans will always inquire, 'Where were you when you heard the news about Earnhardt?'"

A fan and his son express their grief on a banner outside the offices of Dale Earnhardt Incorporated.

What was it about Earnhardt that caused so many people who never even met the man to be catapulted so deeply into mourning? According to April Day of Clearwater, Florida, in *The Tampa Tribune*, "This is a man who cared about everyone. He was NASCAR."

And while fans were left in shock and dismay, asking "why?" and looking for someone or something to blame, they knew the search was futile. "Now is not the time to lay blame. It does not change anything," wrote a fan on *ESPN.com*. "If you can blame it on something, what will it change? And then who wins?" Earnhardt died doing what he loved, and according to John Brawley of Mooresville, North Carolina, "I'm sure if you'd told Dale before the Daytona 500 he would die on the last lap of the race with a chance to win he'd say, 'I'm ready to go.'"

Mooresville Mourns

Even keeping that in mind, this great loss hit his fans hard. However, while fans no longer have their hero, they found that they still do

Across the United States, funeral homes provided memory books for Earnhardt fans to sign to be forwarded to the Earnhardt family.

Fans came to Mooresville, NC, to leave momentos and flowers in Earnhardt's memory.

AP/WWP

have each other. And the signs of this were everywhere. The *CNN Morning News* reported that people flocked to Mooresville, North Carolina, the site of Earnhardt's business and also known as "Race City, USA," some having "literally driven six to 10 hours, some of them overnight, so they could come to this memorial." Greensboro's *News & Record* reported traffic jams outside of Welcome, North Carolina, where Richard Childress Racing (RCR) houses Earnhardt's garage. The newspaper reported that one 15-year-old boy made the pilgrimage to the RCR museum, which is also located in Welcome. He brought with him the American flag that had previously hung on his bedroom wall. The boy placed the flag among the flowers laid at the gate to the museum, a tribute to his American hero.

Tears At Daytona

Outside of the Daytona International Speedway the day after the tragedy, shrines covered the grounds as an airplane circled over the track, trailing a banner that read: "Dale – You were the best of all." Flags bearing the #3 were turned upside down and flown at half staff. Piles of flowers, cards, notes and letters, stuffed animals, photos, candles, and signs graced

> "I didn't go to work today, I just couldn't. It would have been too hard," said one St. Petersburg resident.

Not Giving Up

The next race on the Winston Cup circuit after the Daytona 500 was held at the North Carolina Speedway. Spokesmen for the venue said that fans started calling immediately to suggest memorial tributes and stopped by to leave flowers at the entrance to the speedway. And they bought tickets, too. Fans may be devastated but they understand that the accident was no one's fault and they're not giving up on racing – Earnhardt wouldn't have wanted them to.

the gates and the grounds. A black cross with the number three inside it was also placed on the fence, standing in memory of Earnhardt and as a reminder that, though he is missed here, he has gone on to a peaceful existence. And fans wrote their memories of Earnhardt on poster boards offered by track employees.

Fan Jim Corazza told *The Morning Call* newspaper, "It was a pretty sad scene. There were a couple hundred people and there was almost dead silence."

And it was reported that all throughout Daytona Beach, car headlights could be seen shining brightly for miles around with the "Headlights for Earnhardt" tribute that was the brainchild of several local radio stations.

Whenever tragedies occur, people look to the eyes of children for solace and

Fans write notes in memory of their favorite driver – who piloted the #3 Monte Carlo.

AP/WWP

A vigil in front of the Daytona International Speedway took place the day after the tragedy.

hope for the future. *The New York Times* reported that one young girl, impacted by her father's sense of loss and pain, wrote a poem to memorialize The Man In Black. She read it to her father over the phone before he left Daytona on his way back to his New Jersey home. So moved by the sincerity and truth of his daughter's poem, the man transcribed the girl's words on a large, makeshift plaque and hung it near the entrance to the Daytona USA museum outside the site of the fatal crash. Hanging for all to see were the poignant and reassuring lines, "He died doing what he liked best. Now is time for our hero to rest."

And the fans kept coming. The *Atlanta Journal-Constitution* reported that while on a typical post-race Monday, Daytona USA, a motorsports interactive attraction and speedway, can boast about 2,000 visitors, February 19 saw over 4,000 by mid-day.

Atlanta And Talladega Mourn

Yet Daytona wasn't the only place that fans gathered. The Associated Press reported that about 3,500 people attended the hour-long memorial service held at the Atlanta Motor Speedway on Tuesday, February 20. According to Speedway President Ed Clark, "When we decided to do this about 4 p.m. (Monday), we started getting calls from all over. It's incredible how fast the word got out."

The Associated Press also reported 4,000 attendees at the service held at the International Motor Sports Hall of Fame, which is located next to the Talladega Superspeedway. And funeral homes around the country set up registries for the general public to send their condolences to the Earnhardt family.

Onward To Meet The King

One Charlotte, North Carolina, resident reportedly left a fitting tribute at one of the many Earnhardt shrines around the country. Among the traditional notes and roses, he set down a license plate with a note on the back that read, "Thanks for bringing a good sport to a higher level. Say hello to Elvis."

Hymns At St. Petersburg

The Tampa Tribune gave the account of a memorial held in St. Petersburg, Florida. The turnout to the memorial site was astounding, the entire racing community's heart was broken. "Rarely have so many on one strip of beach remained so reverently quiet as they did Monday night at 6:12 as the final notes of 'Amazing Grace' spread over the gathering crowd of close to 2,000 race fans. They stood with three fingers stretched heavenward, heads bowed on sunlit, tear-stained faces." "This was their makeshift church. They were family. 'Amazing Grace' was their song. Dale Earnhardt their driver." Of course, not

Makeshift memorials to Earnhardt appeared across the country.

everyone adored Earnhardt, but even those who didn't follow his point standings race to race appreciated the impact the veteran racer had on the revolution of NASCAR from small-town sport to national amusement.

Flowers and memorabilia are left at Gateway International Raceway in Illinois.

AP/WWP

President Bush Responds

President George W. Bush, a long time friend of the Earnhardt family, sent his condolences to Teresa, Earnhardt's widow. President Bush, a great sports fan, also sent White House aide Joe Allbaugh to attend the memorial service in Charlotte with the Earnhardt family. Calling his friend "an American icon who made great contributions to his sport," President Bush also remembered the private Earnhardt, the man who was a "down-to-earth, straightforward, plain-spoken fellow."

"Local Boy Done Good"

Earnhardt will be remembered as a ruthless competitor on the tracks and a kind hearted, community-minded gentleman in his private life. He'd do anything for fans, friends and strangers, including visiting the sick in hospitals and giving his time and money to those in need. Fearing that he would be perceived as "soft" and his image on the track would be diminished, Earnhardt never publicized his efforts to make life for those around him just that much easier. "He was a humanitarian," said one fan in mourning outside DEI headquarters in North Carolina. "He gave a lot to the people of Kannapolis. There's a road named after him. He was our local boy done good." All the people outside the headquarters were overcome with grief (some were even too weak to stand), yet there was an understanding. A sign that hung over the memorial site read: "It's hard to lose a hero, but at least we've got the memories."

Life Goes On

Earnhardt's fatal crash left many fans wondering what was next. After two decades of rooting for their favorite driver, what did the future hold? How could there be stock car racing without The Intimidator?

But the week after Daytona, fans everywhere got to see that Earnhardt's legacy wouldn't be leaving any time soon. The 2001 Dura Lube 400 at North Carolina Speedway was a memorable one for anyone lucky enough to see it as Earnhardt's protege Steve Park left with his first career victory.

The day's rain may have held up the race, but it didn't stop Steve Park's #1 Pennzoil Chevrolet from battling neck and neck with Bobby Labonte to take first place. "I started thinking about winning the race and forgot about driving," said Park, "but then I got a kick in the back of the head that reminded me that I needed to stand up on that seat and spin that steering wheel the way Dale has always taught me to do."

Earnhardt's 1980 Monte Carlo at the International Motorsports Hall of Fame has become another memorial to the Winston Cup champ.

During his victory lap, Park waved a black #3 cap through the window, honoring the man who should have been there. "I almost ran into Michael Waltrip there 'cause I couldn't see," said an emotional Park. "I had tears in my eyes."

"It's unfortunate that we didn't have the opportunity to celebrate with Dale," Park said, "but he was there."

He was indeed.

Fans show their love for Earnhardt in many ways.

Best Wishes From A Young Fan

My name is Stacie and I am a fan of one of the greatest race car drivers of all time – Dale Earnhardt. I am only 17, but have been a fan of his since I was 3. While people say to be a true fan, you have to have been there from the start, I know that isn't true, because I was not even born then.

At my house on race day, it is like a major fight about the winner because I love Earnhardt and my Mom likes Jeff Gordon. Dale was the only man I have cheered for and now that he has passed away, I look for Dale Earnhardt Jr. to uphold the name.

I wish Dale Jr. all the luck in the world if he continues to race. I want to tell the rest of his kids that I wish them the best in all they do. To his wife, I wish her all the luck in the world and wish her the best of luck getting through this. And also to all his friends.

We miss Dale Earnhardt dearly.

— Stacie Hastings, Delmar, Delaware, #1 Dale Earnhardt fan

Stacie Hastings is an Earnhardt fan.

Jamie Squire/Allsport

The Fans Speak Out

173

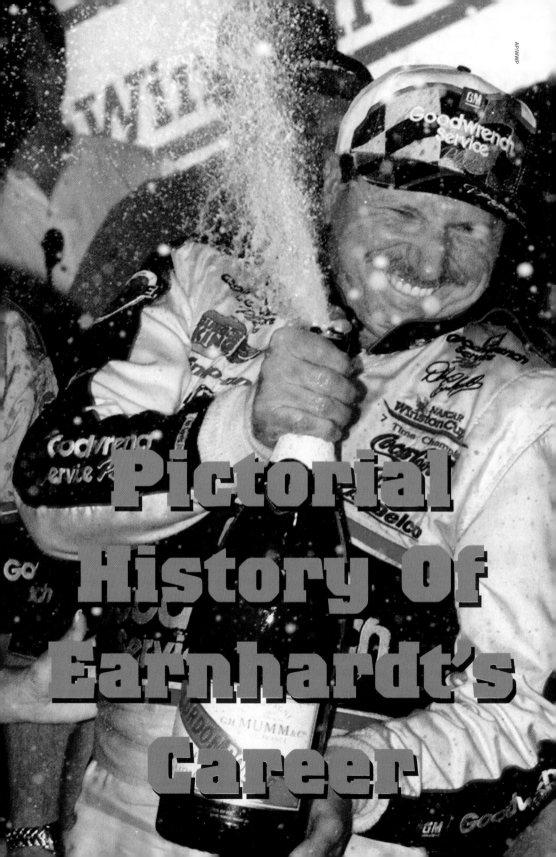

Pictorial History Of Earnhardt's Career

Winston Cup Cars In Action

Dale Earnhardt's career progressed a long way since he first started racing, and so did his cars. In 1969, The Man In Black made his professional racing debut in a 1956 pink Ford Victoria sponsored by a local service center. The engines in it were built by Earnhardt's dad. Earnhardt went on to win his first Winston Cup race in a 1975 RPM Dodge Charger.

In 1978, The Intimidator drove the first of many Chevrolet Monte Carlos and briefly switched to Chevrolet Luminas from 1989 to 1994. But no matter which car he drove, Earnhardt was a winner. His cars took him to victory lane more than 70 times in his career. Pictured here are some of Earnhardt's more memorable Winston Cup cars in action, along with nuggets about his career.

AP-WWP

1979 Crane Cams Chevrolet Monte Carlo

This car took Earnhardt to victory in the Southeastern 500 during his Winston Cup rookie year. It's pictured here at the Firecracker 400.

Bettmann/CORBIS

1982 Wrangler Ford Thunderbird

Earnhardt (#15) crosses the finish line once again, this time in a Ford driven for team owner Bud Moore.

Did You Know?

1982 saw Earnhardt finish the NASCAR season at #12 in the standings, even though he amassed 12 top-ten finishes. The only other year he rounded out the season lower than #8 was 1992, when he also came in at #12 overall.

1988 Goodwrench Chevrolet Monte Carlo

Photo Credit

Teresa gives her husband a kiss after he wins the Busch Clash at the Daytona International Speedway. This car brought Dale victory in three Winston Cup races that year.

AP/WWP

1990 Goodwrench Chevrolet Lumina

During his first full year driving a Chevy Lumina, Dale won nine races, including this victory at the Checker 500.

Andy Lyons/Allsport

1995 Goodwrench Chevrolet Monte Carlo

Back in a Monte Carlo for the first time since 1989, Earnhardt drove this car to victory in five races, including the Brickyard 400. He is seen here at the Daytona 500.

Did You Know?

1995 saw The Man In Black come in at second place at the end of the racing season. He rang up 19 top-five finishes and brought home more than $3 million in winnings.

David Taylor/Allsport

1997 Goodwrench Chevrolet Monte Carlo

This car, shown here at the Interstate Battery 500 in Texas, was involved in the infamous Daytona 500 crash in which Earnhardt left an ambulance to get back into and drive his car.

Craig Jones/Allsport

1997 Goodwrench Plus Chevrolet Monte Carlo

This was Earnhardt's first car to bear the Goodwrench Plus logo. It's seen here at the Bud at the Glen event in New York.

Craig Jones/Allsport

1998 Bass Pro Shops Chevrolet Monte Carlo

Earnhardt's car, co-sponsored by Bass Pro Shops and sporting a special paint scheme, spins out of control at The Winston.

Craig Jones/Allsport

2000 Peter Max Chevrolet Monte Carlo

Earnhardt's car, with a paint scheme designed by pop artist Peter Max, comes around the corner at the Coca Cola 600.

2000 Taz No Bull Chevrolet Monte Carlo

Earnhardt's car is dressed up in a special Taz paint scheme at the Daytona Speedweek. This is an annual event that culminates with the Daytona 500.

Did You Know?

Earnhardt only captured two checkered flags in 2000, but finished in the top ten 24 times. That was good enough to propel The Intimidator into second place at the end of the year.

What Dale Drove

Throughout his career, Earnhardt has driven many different models of cars with different sponsors and paint schemes. Presented here is a chronological list of his Winston Cup cars, with each sponsor, make, model and number.

1975

RPM Dodge Charger (#8)

1976

Army Chevrolet Malibu (#30)
Hy Gain Chevrolet Malibu (#77)

1978

Rod Osterlund Chevrolet
Monte Carlo (#98)

1979

Crane Cams Chevrolet
Monte Carlo (#2)

1980

Mike Curb Oldsmobile 442 (#2)
Mike Curb Wrangler Chevrolet
Monte Carlo (#2)

1981

Wrangler Pontiac (#2)
Wrangler Pontiac (#3)

1982

Wrangler Ford Thunderbird (#15)

1983

Wrangler Ford Thunderbird (#15)

1984

Goodwrench Chevrolet Monte Carlo
(#3, blue trunk)
Goodwrench Chevrolet Monte Carlo
(#3, yellow trunk)

1985

Wrangler Chevrolet Monte Carlo (#3)

1986

Wrangler Chevrolet Monte Carlo (#3)

1987

Wrangler Chevrolet Monte Carlo (#3)

1988

Goodwrench Chevrolet
Monte Carlo (#3)

1989

Goodwrench Chevrolet Lumina (#3)
Goodwrench Chevrolet
    Monte Carlo (#3)

1990

Goodwrench Chevrolet Lumina (#3)

1991

Goodwrench Chevrolet Lumina (#3)

1992

Goodwrench Chevrolet Lumina (#3)

1993

Goodwrench Chevrolet Lumina (#3)

1994

Goodwrench Chevrolet Lumina (#3)

1995

Goodwrench Chevrolet
    Monte Carlo (#3)
Winston Silver Select Chevrolet
    Monte Carlo (#3)

1996

Goodwrench Chevrolet
    Monte Carlo (#3)
Olympics Chevrolet Monte Carlo (#3)

1997

Goodwrench Chevrolet
    Monte Carlo (#3)
Goodwrench Plus Chevrolet
    Monte Carlo (#3)
Wheaties Chevrolet Monte Carlo (#3)

1998

Bass Pro Shops Chevrolet
    Monte Carlo (#3)
Coca-Cola Chevrolet
    Monte Carlo (#3)
Goodwrench Plus Chevrolet
    Monte Carlo (#3)

1999

Goodwrench Plus Chevrolet
    Monte Carlo (#3)
Goodwrench Plus 25th Anniversary
    Chevrolet Monte Carlo (#3)
Goodwrench Plus Chevrolet
    Monte Carlo (#3, Goodwrench
    sign on hood)
Wrangler Colors Chevrolet
    Monte Carlo (#3)

2000

Goodwrench Plus Chevrolet
    Monte Carlo (#3)
Peter Max Chevrolet
    Monte Carlo (#3)
Taz No Bull Chevrolet
    Monte Carlo (#3)

2001

Goodwrench Plus Chevrolet
    Monte Carlo (#3)

Die-Cast Replicas

Earnhardt fans everywhere can show their loyalty to him by collecting the vast number of die-cast cars that have been made in his honor. These cars, some of which are shown below, span his entire career.

1956 Ford Victoria

69-78

1978 Rod Osterlund Chevrolet Monte Carlo

1982 Wrangler Ford Thunderbird

1984 Wrangler Chevrolet Monte Carlo

82-84

1984 Wrangler Chevrolet Monte Carlo

1986 Wrangler Chevrolet Monte Carlo

86-88

1988 Goodwrench Chevrolet Monte Carlo

93-96

1995 Goodwrench
Chevrolet Monte Carlo

1993 Goodwrench
Chevrolet Lumina

1995 Winston Silver
Select Chevrolet
Monte Carlo

1996 Olympics
Chevrolet Monte Carlo

1997 Wheaties
Chevrolet Monte Carlo

97-99

1998 Bass Pro
Shops Chevrolet
Monte Carlo

1999 Wrangler Colors
Chevrolet Monte Carlo

2000

2000 Taz No Bull Chevrolet
Monte Carlo

2000 Goodwrench Plus
Chevrolet Monte Carlo

Sponsors Through The Years

Sponsors are the financial lifeline of every driver in NASCAR. Corporations pay big bucks to have their company name and logo emblazoned across the hood of a top driver's car, which has often been referred to as "a moving billboard." Prime real estate on a car is the hood, which is worth between $7 and $12 million in sponsorship dollars but, for a mere $75,000, your company decal can be placed on the column between the side windows. This money is used to pay for the expenses of keeping a top driver supplied with the most up-to-date equipment and staffed with the most talented personnel.

Mike Curb Productions – 1980

Earnhardt and his #2 Mike Curb car make a pit stop.

One of Earnhardt's very first sponsors was Mike Curb, who started out as a record producer in California and who also happened to love NASCAR. After sponsoring Earnhardt, he sponsored Richard Petty. In 1984, he invited President Ronald Reagan to watch Petty win the Daytona 500. Curb currently owns a car driven by Jay Sauter.

Wrangler – 1980-1987

Earnhardt's Wrangler Ford Thunderbird is ready to race.

Earnhardt's relationship with Wrangler lasted for almost eight years, during which time he earned his tough-guy reputation. Wrangler is still involved with DEI as an associate sponsor for driver Steve Park.

Goodwrench – 1988-1997

Bill Frakes/Allsport

Earnhardt's crew rushes to get his
Goodwrench Chevy back on the track.

The Man In Black made his first appearance with a paint scheme sporting the black-and-white Goodwrench logo in 1988.

Wheaties - 1997

Wheaties, the "Breakfast of Champions," co-sponsored Earnhardt's car in 1997 for the Winston Select. The bright-orange car certainly drew attention and corresponded with Earnhardt's earlier appearance on the Wheaties cereal box.

Bass Pro Shops - 1998

Karl DeBlaker/Allsport

Earnhardt's Bass Pro Shops car gets some
quick pit service at The Winston.

What better sponsor is there for an outdoorsman like Earnhardt, than Bass Pro Shops? This supplier of fishing, hunting and camping supplies co-sponsored his car for the Winston Select in 1998.

Goodwrench Service Plus – 1997-2001

Earnhardt finished up his career driving
a Goodwrench Service Plus car.

Midway through the 1997 NASCAR season, Goodwrench added the word "Plus" to their name "Goodwrench Service." And Earnhardt, in an advertising campaign to publicize the improved service at GM shops, starred in a television spot in which he asks his pit crew if their work is guaranteed. One of the crew members responds with, "Are you kidding? Do you think this is GM Goodwrench Service Plus?" Goodwrench remained an Earnhardt sponsor for 14 years.

FAN CHECKERBEE GUIDE

Photo Index

U se this index to find photographs of individuals and racetracks depicted in this book. Pages are listed in numerical order.